# BUSINESS PLANNING
# FOR THE BOARD

# Business Planning
# for the Board

Editor: HUGH BUCKNER

*First published in Britain in 1971 by Gower Press Limited
140 Great Portland Street, London WIN 5TA*

© *Gower Press Limited 1971*

*ISBN 0 7161 0061 4*

*Set in 10 on 12 point Times and Printed in England by
A Wheaton & Co, Exeter*

# Contents

# Illustrations

# Introduction

*by Hugh Buckner*

Probably no other word in business communication is closer to losing its intended meaning than "planning." This can be seen in the rate at which new prefixes are added in an attempt to retain the original idea. First "long range" was added. As this became confused with forecasting it fell into disuse. Corporate planning and formal planning followed in quick succession. To a large extent this debasement parallels the history of the marketing concept. Marketing started as an outlook to be applied to all company operations, internal as well as external. Today in many companies it has come to be regarded simply as the new jargon for the sales activity. This erosion of a powerful new concept until it fits the comfortable old approach is in danger of occurring with planning. It must be prevented.

## Relationship between objectives and planning

Much of the available literature has aided this debasement. The first step in many planning approaches is stated to be the setting of objectives, but objectives should arise as a result of planning: they should not form the starting point. Planning is the activity that leads to specific objectives being chosen, as much as it is the scheduling and budgeting of the actions needed to make the objectives become reality.

Corporate objectives are, of course, derived from those of the persons who comprise the company but individuals seldom have a single objective on any point. Most often a person embraces within himself multiple and often conflicting aims. On separate days, depending on the environment, different ideas are ascendant. Even in the rare company where there is only one policy maker, this constant changing of importance among conflicting objectives makes for corporate confusions. If several policy makers are working together in a political atmosphere, line managers cannot discern a meaningful purpose in the firm's development. If business planning is to be a real tool to fashion the corporate future it needs to be written. Only then can the reasoning be clear to all over a period of time.

The written planning process becomes retraceable and is also more comprehensive than that derived from the intuitive approach. It forces managers to think ahead in an organised way and to consider alternatives when they may be guilty of tunnel vision. It helps to avoid errors which often occur when, for example, a new product or service is introduced without a comprehensive look at the business situation. These problems are all too real in most businesses. The following are typical illustrations:

**1** An engineering company developed a hydrostatic transmission for the military and then invested heavily in promoting it for the civilian vehicle markets before realising, when the sales failed to materialise, the relatively low cost of a gearbox.
**2** A large travel agency undertook major regional expansion largely because of the profitability of its London business. The new operations proved only marginally profitable. Shortly afterwards, the London operations profitability started to fall, and only then was it realised just how important, to the London operation, had been the group travel business coming from the film industry. This film industry group travel, which had started to decline, had never existed in the regions. There had, therefore, never been a viable reason for the regional expansion.

Planning can be defined simply without the need for prefixes: planning is retraceable reasoning as to why a company has specific aims, what these aims are and how they are to be achieved.

## Why planning is necessary

The importance of planning today derives from continuing changes in the business environment. For many companies, the major external reason is the continuing rate of technical change, which has an important effect on product life and development times. The time over which a successful product earns major profits is declining. At the same time the product probably costs more to develop than its predecessor. Thus a greater investment needs to be recovered over a shorter time. Companies can no longer allow themselves the luxury of compensating for initial errors by changes introduced after the product is launched. The time involved in the changes will bite increasingly into the time the product has to repay the investment and risk in undertaking it.

An additional reason for sound business planning is the increasing rate of competitive change. A direct competitor is now as likely to be from Japan as from Birmingham. The record of performance shows companies to have been neither opportunistic nor expansive in the face of this change which has hit most companies' export as well as home markets.

Competition from alternatives has also arisen. Sales of metal products decline as plastic and concrete increases. Again, with individuals now well past survival level in incomes, competition is no longer only among similar products. At any one time their purchasing decision may embrace very different products for different purposes. A packaged holiday may compete directly with a new car. The customer chooses in terms of which alternative seems to offer the highest value. In the same way, corporate buyers with a wealth of alternatives available increasingly look at the effect on the total of one alternative against another rather than examining straight price comparisons. Only by planning a company's whole effort to be value-oriented can the threat of competition be reduced.

The number of technical disciplines involved in successfully producing a product is also increasing and it is frequently impossible for one man to appreciate all the important factors. As a result, an individual acting alone can often miss a factor of crucial importance. This can be seen in the number of new products which, although interesting developments, prove to be commercially useless. They may for instance be a technical advance in the "wrong" direction or they may have only small markets. In this situation innovation often becomes stifled.

A formal plan aids corporate creativity in two main ways:

**1** By identifying clearly the opportunities and alternatives, it allows many persons from differing disciplines in the company to play a part in evolving the plan. As a result the plan is both sounder in itself and also represents an agreed and understood direction.
**2** By locating the crucial factors, a company can bring its creative talent, wherever it lies, to bear on specified aspects. The crucial factors

are those where a small change has a large effect on the business. For example, in some industries a small volume increase in sales produces a disproportionate increase in profits. Or a small increase in influence over a distribution channel starts a chain of events which leads to total domination. This concentration of innovative talent does not increase the frequency of innovation but it does mean that innovation, when it occurs, is more likely to be of major importance to the company.

Large companies need a business plan that enables them to "think big." Large and even medium companies are increasingly finding that size is a competitive disadvantage. Despite much-vaunted reasons for larger companies, there is no evidence that economies of scale have been achieved. The results of an analysis carried out by the *Financial Times* was as shown in the table below.

| COMPANY SALES £ MILLION | NO. OF COMPANIES | AVERAGE PROFITS AS PERCENTAGE OF TOTAL ASSETS |
|---|---|---|
| Under 1 | 12 | 13.17 |
| 1–2 | 26 | 14.35 |
| 2–4 | 38 | 11.06 |
| 4–8 | 65 | 11.07 |
| 8–16 | 40 | 11.94 |
| 16–32 | 43 | 9.73 |
| 32–64 | 37 | 10.17 |
| 64–128 | 22 | 10.20 |
| 128–256 | 18 | 9.12 |
| 256 or more | 12 | 11.26 |
| All groups | 313 | 11.08 |

TABLE 1   COMPARATIVE PROFITABILITY OF LARGE AND SMALL COMPANIES

It can be seen that companies under £1 000 000 sales have returns on assets of 13 per cent and companies with sales over £256 000 000 have returns of 11 per cent. These larger companies are either rated by their customers (in terms of willingness to pay a reasonable price) as less effective than the smaller companies or they are less efficient in themselves. The difficulty appears to be the failure of large companies to be entrepreneurial. With growth they move into a protective-reactive stage where their resources are moved to meet each market change as if it were a threat.

A company today must consciously plan its human skills to be in line with its other investments. Since the Second World War and with the passing of the *industrial revolution* and *mass production* phases business has moved into the *mass consumption* phase. Success has increasingly revolved around customer-satisfying intangibles rather than products. Whether it is process know-how in the manufacture of a product or direct applications engineering, it is problem solving for the customer that creates the environment in which product price is secondary. The application of knowledge in the form of unique skills is now the major asset of a company and must rank with all tangible resources in assessment.

### Difference between plans and forecasts

It is often difficult to appreciate the value of planning when the work is so confused with choosing a target, forecasting, and other such activities. Probably the only point which can be made about a forecast which states that a product will achieve a specific sales value in five years' time is that it is unlikely to happen. If it did happen it would probably be a low profit situation. This is because such predictability would almost by itself ensure that the competition was severe. This difficulty in forecasting five years ahead can be proved in any company. A simple look backwards over the recent past would show that many surprises occurred which played a major part in determining where the company is today. The same situation will occur in future.

In contrast with forecasting, planning is ideally a search into the future to see how the company can situate itself *now* to take advantage of whatever *may happen* tomorrow.

Budget forecasts derived from a projection of future markets are not, therefore, plans. They are what they say they are—forecasts. This misconception of planning is widespread. Even in the *Harvard Business Review* of September–October 1970, an article appeared discussing "The accuracy of long range planning." What was actually discussed was the accuracy of business forecasting. Companies who exceeded their forecasts (good planning?) were considered as inaccurate as those who failed to reach them.

The main problem is that overemphasis on forecasting tends to limit the vision of those producing the business plan. The more detailed the forecasts that are required or used the more nearly those producing the plan need to adhere to projecting the past. All forms of forecasting are based on extrapolation of the past. If those formulating the business plans could break free from extrapolating the past and consider the alternatives to their present actions and forms of operating, they would have a clearer idea of how they could act to secure the future whatever it turns out to be.

The examples are legion of plans which are simply projections ahead of the present activities. They consist of page after page of detailed breakdowns of costs and personnel requirements. Too many managers find it impossible to generate alternatives and can view the future only as a continuation of the past with perhaps some minor modifications. A typical example is the leading British company which developed a plan for part of its business in which four strategies were considered. Some of its action features were:

*Strategy* 1
1    Develop the distributive structure to accommodate sales of £2 250 000 in 1971 rising to £3 150 000 in 1975
2    Screen all outlets and eliminate those not capable of £250 000 a year
3    Upgrade the product by adding a new model 15 per cent in price/performance above the present range and eliminate lowest price model
4    Advertising budget to be £60 000 per annum
5    Sales emphasis and promotional mix to remain unchanged

*Strategy* 2
Same as strategy 1 but increased sales of £2 500 000 in 1971 rising to £3 500 000 in 1975. Increase advertising budget to £70 000.

*Strategy* 3
Same as strategy 1 but increased sales of £2 750 000 in 1971 rising to £3 750 000 in 1975. Increase advertising budget to £80 000.

*Strategy* 4
Same as strategy 1 but increased sales of £3 000 000 in 1971 to £4 200 000 by 1975. Increase advertising budget to £95 000.

The plan was, of course, more detailed than the above. It was also sound as far as it went. It certainly provided management with an idea of the investment needed and results to be expected over a range of sales levels. The horrifying aspect is that the company believed itself to have four alternatives instead of one alternative with four levels of involvement.

Those undertaking business planning will find their greatest challenge in endeavouring to locate the alternative to the current operations. In doing this the emphasis must be on creativity. The chance for higher profits lies in operations where a company can be to some extent unique. A company never makes above-average profit from a machine, a factory, or a product. It is from the intangibles of exclusiveness, creativity, knowhow and understanding of the customer's problems that above-average profits arise. There are always alternative strategies and it is essential in planning to identify them.

### Formulating alternative strategies

In any company alternative strategies can be located by examining each of the separate factors in the business in the light of the purpose of strategy itself. Two major purposes can be recognised in strategic decision making and, therefore, need to be considered when examining alternatives.

First, the purpose of strategic action is to position the businesses of the company so that the types of decisions, the areas of uncertainty, the opportunities and the growth forces acting on the company are the most favourable. In this sense strategy is concerned with the types of business to be in and the extent to which the company should be committed to each type. Thus strategy positions the company so that, ideally, it benefits from whatever happens tomorrow. The aims of this type of strategy are:

1 Selecting business areas of inherent advantage for the company, such as those it is good at
2 Selecting operating modes of inherent advantage for the company, such as meeting competition on its own ground
3 Positioning the company within the mainstream of economic activity so as to serve growth markets
4 Creating opportunity by innovating alternatives, leading to attack from unexpected directions
5 Setting meaningful goals and determining ways in which they can be achieved to create a unity of purpose and drive

6      Identifying the directions for research and development, such as products, distribution channels and so on

Naturally, each company already has a strategy. It may be unexpressed or even unrealised. Many companies' existing strategies generate only low profits because, for example, the product or service offered is similar to that of the competition. It is not suggested that this situation can be altered immediately. But it is the purpose of strategic action to move the company slowly toward controlling its own profit environment.

The second major purpose of strategic decision making is to provide a framework for thought which is to be applied as the future unfolds and opportunities occur. Thus strategy in this sense is not in itself a specific statement of physical action but a set of ground rules for thinking which are to be applied to situations which are as yet unknown. This is the real business position. For all companies the future will contain surprises and plans will require modification. The rules for such modification are strategy. With many men in a company taking important decisions over time it is vital that the same ground rules are applied to each judgement. In this sense, therefore, strategy can be thought of as:

1      Distinctiveness in concept of the business, which means choosing factors in which the company intends to be unique, such as innovation or style or volume of production
2      Basic policies on:
   (a) Investment
   (b) Forms of growth
   (c) Personnel
   (d) Quality/cost
   (e) Proprietary positions sought
3      Corporate goals:
   (a) Quantitative targets
   (b) Qualitative basic objectives for each prime part of the company

Despite the importance of planning, few companies have strategies which are distinctive and understood by all decision makers. In many cases strategy is confused with the tactics of budgeting and investment appraisal. As a result, planning becomes inflexible in dealing with the very purpose of strategy—uncertainty.

## A system for business planning

Planning systems provide an essential order of approach to developing a complete understanding of a company's likely results, alternatives and opportunities. To enable one unified assessment to be made of the potential for the company in each business area the plan needs to:

1    Supply a logical base for thinking
2    Ensure that comprehensive consideration is given to each alternative
3    Keep the necessary recycling of the parts of the plan to a minimum
4    Be practical, workable and allow business planning to grow naturally as a function within the company

At the same time, the planning system should not in the early stages place too much emphasis on the physical counting of people, resources, and end targets. Although such activities are necessary to the task of scheduling, they can too easily become confused with the total act of planning, leading to a consequent overemphasis on forecasting to the detriment of creativity. Planners should not shrink from identifying good opportunities which cannot be quantified fully.

One point is especially important when using planning systems. Naturally such systems consist of a series of steps connected together. Each step may itself involve many important questions. There is, therefore, a danger of planning becoming similar to the comprehensive filling-in of a questionnaire with equal importance being given to each step. While all aspects should be considered, the major portion of time should be spent in identifying and examining those factors which are crucial to success. Emphasis should then be placed on these factors.

One basic system for planning is shown in Figure 1. Most companies who have not previously planned formally will find it difficult to develop a full formal plan in one annual cycle. Probably as a first stage they should draw up a sales forecast and develop detailed operational budgets from it. This first sales forecast should represent the best estimate of future sales in the absence of major changes such as of policy, introduction of new products or the development of new markets. Thus, the operational budgets derived from the forecast will represent the current *momentum* of the company.

At this stage, detailed discussions should be held with each line manager, ranging freely over all aspects of the business and so generating

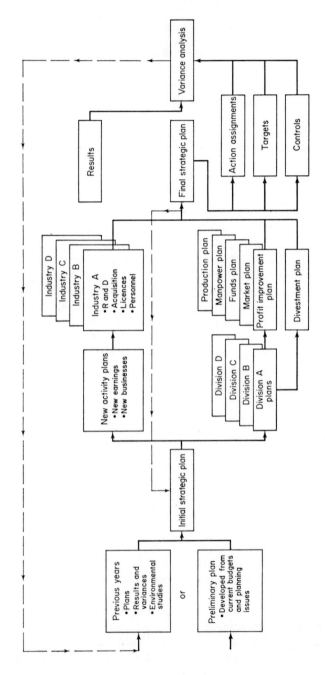

FIGURE 1 BASIC SYSTEM FOR PLANNING

"issues." The result of acting on each issue, including the cash flows in and out, can then be computed in terms of its effect on the momentum line budget forecast. Thus for each issue a cost/benefit to the company can be identified.

It is usual to find that only a small number of the issues affect the company's future significantly. The remainder can be discarded. The significant issues should now be subjected to more detailed analysis and discussion among policy makers. The momentum line budget forecasts, amended to include actions on those issues accepted, forms the provisional plan, which leads directly into the full planning cycle for the following year.

Many companies' plans are summations of the separate plans of divisions or other operating groups. This is so called *bottom-up* planning. It is vital, however, for the corporate headquarters to draft the initial strategic plan. To avoid doing so is to make the headquarters into an investment rather than operating organisation. Only if *top-down* planning exists can decisions, such as to expand one division at the expense of another, be taken. It is quite realistic to imagine a situation in which a division which can meet standard investment criteria may nevertheless be told to hold back growth so as to throw off cash to aid in expansion elsewhere. The headquarters assess what is required from each division by considering their previous years' plans and performance, together with new opportunities, developments and the headquarters' objectives. This will result in initial targets for each division and probably also some targets for developing new sources of earnings.

Each division now determines in detail how it can most nearly accomplish the requirements of the initial strategic plan. At this stage, there will certainly be some reconsideration of the original strategy. Finally, however, agreement will be reached and line managers will commit themselves to achieving their plans. These taken together will form the final strategic plan.

The actions needed to bring all aspects of the plan to fruition must be delegated, as personal objectives, to individuals in the organisation. Each action should have a specified *action assignee* together with budgets and expected results. Control stages should be specified and the form of control and *control assignee* stated. Company personnel need to see that achievement of the plan is one of the major ways in which they will be assessed as individuals. Finally, actual performance month by month needs to be compared with the plan and any developing variances countered.

## How to use this book

Each chapter in this book is a separate contribution by a specialist practitioner in his field. While business planning could properly be related to all business operations, the need for conciseness demanded that the scope of the book be limited to the vital areas. This has enabled the authors to be as detailed as they feel necessary.

The book, therefore, concentrates on the development of the planning organisation and the planning process (Chapter 1) together with the dynamic areas of business planning:

1      Marketing
2      New products
3      Manpower planning
4      Acquisitions
5      Financial planning

Appendix 1 contains an initial appraisal check list which summarises many of the factors discussed in the chapters.

It is probable that two readings of the book are necessary for those using it as a working guide. The first should identify the company's current strengths and weaknesses, opportunities and threats. This is an audit of the current position. The second reading evaluates the alternatives that are open to the company in terms of different approaches rather than specific opportunities. Following these two stages, the beginnings of objective setting can take place, leading naturally to schedules, budgets and action assignments for specific individuals.

# ONE

# The Planning Process

*by L B Pinnell*

The organisation of formalised comprehensive planning for a business is important because, while good organisation makes successful planning possible, bad organisation is guaranteed to ensure failure even though the planning procedures themselves may have been very carefully devised. There have been many studies of planning organisation designed to find out what ingredients seem to be essential to success.

### 1:1 Requirements for successful planning

Business planning has to be seen as the inescapable responsibility of the chief executive and board, because of their obvious duty to marshal all the assets of the company (human, physical and financial) in the interests of shareholders, customers, employees and the community generally. It follows that success in planning requires not only the full support of the chief executive and board, but also their direct involvement. Should planning be thought of as an activity to be left solely to specialists or back-room boys, however gifted, with the directors playing no active part, the result will eventually be disillusionment and failure. Only at board level is there the power to define the major objectives to be achieved and the policies to be followed and the power to take decisions from among the alternative courses available.

A second requirement for a successful planning organisation is to ensure that senior line management is actively involved. Line management is held responsible for executing agreed plans and for achieving the required results. They will be more successful in doing this if they have personally contributed to creating the plan so that the proposals in it are their own. If they have not been personally involved and the plan is the brain-child of a staff man who attempts to sell it to the line managers, the chances of successfully implementing the plan are greatly reduced. Resistance may be created partly because the plan itself, however carefully conceived, may be regarded as evidence of a bid for power at the expense of the existing hierarchy of managers. Even if this view is mistaken, the damage will have been done.

The third requirement for success is to provide in the organisation the specialist planning assistance which is genuinely needed by the board, the chief executive and the line management. The amount of assistance needed will range from nothing at all in the smallest organisations to massive specialist departments in the largest. We can now translate these general ideas into specific organisational terms.

### 1:2  Structure of planning activity

In a medium-sized company the individuals mainly involved in business planning might be as in Figure 1:1. In this example there are no full time planning staff but as the organisation grows in size and complexity the amount of planning assistance needed may justify the appointment of managers and/or specialists on a part- or full-time basis. Initially the main assistance tends to come from the accounting departments, but the organisation structure might eventually become something like that in Figure 1:2.

A study of twenty-four large British companies late in 1967 published by the British Institute of Management (*Is Corporate Planning Necessary?*) showed that only a minority had established full-time central

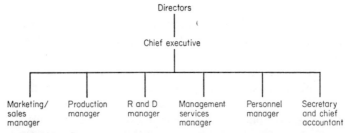

FIGURE 1:1  PERSONNEL MAINLY INVOLVED IN
BUSINESS    PLANNING    OF    MEDIUM-SIZED
COMPANY

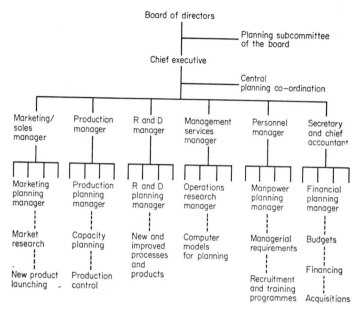

FIGURE 1:2 ORGANISATIONAL STRUCTURE OF
PLANNING STAFF IN LARGE COMPANY

planning activities. Only four of the companies had planning departments, one of these having thirty staff and the other three only five or
six each. In three companies there were planning staff rather than departments. In all the other companies accounting staff usually did whatever
was necessary on a central basis in connection with formalised planning.

Where full time central planning staff exist, the director or manager
in charge generally reports directly to the chief executive or to a group
of directors specifically concerned with policy matters. A study by Mr P
Irving into the development of organised planning in major UK
companies has shown that only four out of twenty-seven full-time professional planners were board members. A third of the twenty-seven
had a background in economics or finance, one in nine came from
marketing and the remainder from an extremely varied background in
both staff and line functions.

The smallest conceivable full-time central planning activity is unlikely
to cost less than £10 000 a year, taking into account the need to involve
line management. At the other extreme the development of complex
planning systems utilising computers on a large scale could involve a

major investment in systems analysis and programming amounting perhaps to £250 000 or more, in addition to staff and computer running costs thereafter perhaps reaching or exceeding £100 000 a year.

## 1:3   Essential steps in business planning

There is no single form of business planning organisation which can be generally copied. In devising a planning organisation the important point is to list the essential responsibilities which need to be carried out by someone, and then consider how to allocate the tasks. The following are some of the essential activities:

**1**  Define how planning is to be done and ensure that the agreed procedures are followed. This is a function of the planning coordinator where he exists.

**2**  Create a statement of overall strategy which defines the main aims of the business in respect of its type of activity and future profitability. This is ultimately a board responsibility.

**3**  Study the costs and benefits of alternative ways of achieving these aims, including the development of new opportunities in products, markets or production processes.

**4**  Make decisions as to which of the alternative courses to follow. This is always the board's responsibility.

**5**  Create action programmes which define how each of the major management functions (sales, production, distribution, personnel, research and development) will implement the decisions made, what overall results will be achieved by the organisation, and what overall resources it will need.

**6**  Ensure implementation of the action programmes by the adoption of appropriate targets for all managers coupled with review of their subsequent performance.

Subsequent sections of this chapter explore these activities in greater detail.

## 1:4   Framing company strategy

Three hundred years ago the word strategy appeared in military literature to describe the kind of thinking which enabled a general to achieve victory on the battlefield. Successful leadership in this sense was seen as an art rather than a science because so many factors in the battle were outside his control. Nevertheless, it was accepted that there were rules for victory in war which would repay study. In business, much strategic thinking is intuitive and follows unwritten rules but there is a growing body of literature which suggests that a logical step-by-step approach can usefully be followed. The aim, of course, is to find out how to compete successfully in the future. In particular, many businesses want to establish how to achieve "victory" against competitors much larger and apparently more powerful than themselves.

*Diagnosing the current situation.* A first step in a procedure for framing a strategy is to decide how the competitive battle is now going and what will happen to the business if events develop as seems probable. The sales trend can be forecast, bearing in mind the size of the market, competitors' probable activities, the effects of technological change and so on. Estimates can be made of the likely course of future selling prices and costs and the profit levels that seem probable over the next few years. Will profits be increasing, static or declining? What will be the return on the capital invested in the business and what sort of income and share value can be offered to shareholders, looking ahead perhaps five years? All these points are discussed in the following chapters.

The answers may be reassuring on all counts. It may seem that the competitive battle is already being won and that competition will be no real threat for years to come. Businesses in this fortunate position will feel they already have a successful strategy. What matters for them is the operational plan to continue to expand as before, to ensure that sales and profits continue their upward path.

Other businesses may not feel content with the picture of the future which they see before them. Perhaps they find themselves in a declining or static market in which falling profit margins cannot be corrected by selling price increases because that will simply enable competitors to increase their market share. It seems certain that such a business must change its activities if it is to survive in the long run. The question is what changes to make, how and when?

*Investigating the competition.* Reverting to the military analogy, it is desirable to fight the enemy of one's choice on a battlefield also of one's choice. Who is it that the business wants to compete against and in what products, services or markets does it choose to compete in future, so as to give itself the best chance of success?

Knowing the competition in this way aids recognition of the crucial point at which force can be brought to bear. Perhaps a gap can be

found in the competitor's product line, either in terms of price or performance, which our company can fill. It may be possible to find an
important customer who gives a competitor considerable business
but appears to be dissatisfied. Has this customer a need, at present not
met, which our company could supply? Alternatively, is there a competitor in financial difficulty, whose position can be exploited because he
cannot match our company's capital expenditure on modern production
equipment?

The essence of this approach is to define the enemy's weaknesses and
then go on to consider how they can be exploited. The third step in the
procedure therefore is a long hard look at our company's strengths so as
to identify which of them may provide the required advantages.

If important gaps in a competitor's product line are found, has our
company the technical ability to develop the missing articles? If a
competitor is weak in salesmanship, is sufficiently strong sales management available to us to organise and lead a greatly expanded sales force?
If he is short of finance for capital expenditure on modern equipment,
is surplus cash available to us in the required amounts? If not, is our company in a better position to us to obtain new funds than the competitor?

At this stage also it must be decided whether competition poses any
threats to our company's future position. Is any competitor building
modern production capacity with lower costs? Is he extending his distribution system to shorten his delivery lead-times below what the
company can offer? What defensive action should be taken?

In completing this procedure for analysing the strengths and weaknesses of our company and its competitors, an attempt should be made to
envisage the possible reactions by competitors to company policy. Are
they likely to counter-attack and so discount a hoped-for advantage?
Or can a type of action be devised which they cannot effectively oppose?
The latter, obviously, could give our company a permanently stronger
position.

*Setting out the policy.* At this point a strategic plan is beginning to take
shape and it will be found worth while to create a document setting
out the policy of our company on the following issues:

**1**  The type of business it intends to engage in, defined in terms of the
customer needs it proposes to meet, the range of products and/or
services it proposes to supply, and the extent to which it will vertically
integrate backward (to the raw material) or forward (to the customer).

**2**  The geographical markets in which the company proposes to operate, such as particular types of towns or regions of the country, and what overseas markets (if any) it considers it should penetrate.

3  The position aimed at in these markets in terms of market share.

4  The resources to be made available in respect of capital funds for expansion.

5  The return on investment required both from new projects and from the business as a whole in future years.

This statement, when discussed and agreed with the board of directors, will provide guidelines to top management who will be investigating and proposing particular projects for approval by the board in the future. To continue this discussion of the planning process let us assume that the above has been carried out. That is that the company has been examined in the manner as set out above. As a result of this analysis we will have a number of alternatives ranging from major differing strategies to perhaps minor changes in operation programmes.

### 1:5  Procedures for evaluating alternatives and decision making

We will assume that each major alternative for the company's policy or strategy has been agreed and that each calls for growth in particular products and geographical areas in order to achieve a stated return on the capital invested.

We will also assume that detailed investigations into various projects are under way and several appear to offer returns on invested capital well above the minimum needed. How are choices to be made if the financial resources available are not large enough to permit approval of the schemes put forward?

An effective approach is to analyse the various opportunities for development under the following headings:

1  The objectives—what is the required result that makes the project desirable? Why is a decision necessary?

2  What further alternative projects could achieve the same result? For each required objective, there may be half a dozen or more projects available. These can be systematically listed by collecting the results of the investigations and gathering the opinions of senior managers. The possible types of project may include the following:

(a)  Developing and selling a new product

(b)  Penetrating a new market with existing products

(c)  Developing a superior production process

(*d*) Changes in the size and/or location of company plants

(*e*) Closing down an unprofitable activity

(*f*) Acquiring or merging with a competitor.

**3** Which one of these possible alternative projects is preferred, and why? The key here is to consider each possible course of action in turn and identify the probable costs and benefits of each. Sometimes much detailed investigation will be necessary, involving market research, project engineers, accountants and others before essential financial data can be collected which points to a particular course of action as "preferred." In other cases, however, this may be unnecessary because the crucial advantages or disadvantages can be discovered without elaborate analytical studies.

**4** When is a decision needed? Possibly only a small percentage of the preferred courses will require a decision in the near future. Other decisions may not be needed for two or three years, and it is not only unnecessary but also undesirable to bring forward the decision date because in the meantime more information may be obtained which may enable a better decision to be made later on. Nevertheless, it is valuable to agree on the decision dates now, so that everyone is reminded of the necessity for making decisions in time. Failure to make a decision is, of course, a decision to do nothing.

There is a further advantage in listing pending decisions in this way. A particular decision today may prevent or force some other decision a year or two later, which may not be in the best interests of the company. Those consequences must be appreciated now, before final decisions are made. An example of the kind of analysis suggested above is shown in Figure 1:3.

Let us assume that many of these statements have been collected, which means that lists have been made of the objectives, the alternative courses of action, the probable costs, benefits, advantages and disadvantages of each, the preferred courses and the dates when decisions are needed. How are these to be used for decision making?

A method must be found whereby all this thinking is consolidated so that the main problems can be seen together. Consolidation itself is not difficult. If the thinking described above has been set out in a logical step-by-step way, a report can be drawn up which lists all the objectives, alternative courses, preferred courses and dates for decisions. If this is presented in sequence of decision dates it will focus attention on the courses requiring decisions in the next six to twelve months and thus help identify priorities.

| Objective | Alternative courses | | Preferred | When decision required | Comments |
|---|---|---|---|---|---|
| | Discarded | Open | | | |
| 1 To meet increased demand for product X in 1973 and maintain market share at 30 per cent | 1(a) Purchase from other suppliers | | | | 1 (a) Product quality unreliable and cost 20 per cent higher |
| | 1(b) Takeover of another supplier | | | | 1(b) Major shareholders will not sell |
| | | 1(c) Expand capacity on new site | | | (c) Present site adequate for next 25 years. New site would duplicate management requirements |
| | | 1(d) Expand capacity on existing site: | | | |
| | | (i) Using y process | | | 1(d)(i) Unsuitable for long runs required |
| | | (ii) Using new $Z_1$ process | | | 1(d)(ii) Meets need for long runs but may be obsoleted next year by $Z_2$ process |
| | | (iii) Using new $Z_2$ process | | | 1(d)(iii) Lower cost operation than $Z_1$ process but proving trials not complete until 1972 |
| | | (iv) Continue using existing process with maximum improvement in throughput and yield until $Z_2$ process proved | 1 (d)(iv) | 1st quarter 1971 | 1(d)(iv) Significant improvements believed achievable by R and D and operations research within 6 months. Cost of 6 month programme £25 000. Can start April 1971 |

FIGURE 1:3  EXTRACT FROM LIST OF PENDING DECISIONS

A ranking system can be devised which lists the objectives of the various projects in some sequence of desirability. How do the aims of each project compare with the overall policies and strategy as laid down earlier? Some projects may appear essential on broad policy grounds, while others seem less relevant to the overall objectives or even contrary to them. The question must also be asked whether the schemes put forward are sufficient in total to carry out the required strategy. Is there a serious gap and, if so, where is it? This gap could be in terms of insufficient profits or a declining strength such as patent expiry. Further studies will be needed to find out how such a gap can be closed.

For many organisations, the main or only criterion for ranking projects will be in terms of the expected return on the investment, and in these cases this information should be provided for all preferred courses in the list. The calculations of returns submitted will need to be vetted for accuracy and completeness. How carefully have the computations been done? What assumptions have been made about the market and the company's share of it? Has inflation been allowed for? Do the capital costs include adequate provision for working capital? Does the profit estimate make any allowance for risk?

When this vetting has been done, an analysis can be drawn up of additional investment and additional profit from each preferred course. This will indicate which projects will generate cash most quickly, which will absorb it most quickly, and which will most rapidly improve the return on capital employed in the company. This list can be issued to the board whenever they are considering capital projects put before them, and will help them in choosing between the alternative schemes, although judgement and intuition can never be replaced by purely mathematical formulae.

At any one moment the list of preferred courses will include schemes which are at a very early stage of consideration and which have not yet been financially evaluated. Decisions on these will still be some way off but their inclusion in the list allows confirmation that these projects should (or should not) be the subject of detailed financial assessment in future. Strategic planning is a continuous activity and the lists of alternative courses need to be kept up to date.

## 1:6   Framing action programmes

The purpose of the action programme is to define how the major management functions will implement the decisions made, and generally make progress in line with the strategic plan for the business.

From a planning viewpoint the most clearcut responsibilities will arise in the case of major capital projects, possibly involving expenditures of many millions of pounds. The original proposal for the project which represented a *preferred course* has, we assume, been approved. If this was thoroughly documented, incorporating detailed market studies, engineering specifications for the plant and buildings and complete financial evaluations of capital cost, operating cost and sales revenues, this will in itself describe an operational plan. It will define in detail the action to be taken and results to be achieved by a major management function, for example the team of engineers responsible for building and commissioning the new works.

What we are more concerned with in this chapter is the role of management in planning to achieve an important business objective such as profit improvement through co-ordinated action in each of the major management functions, such as sales, manufacturing, distribution, research and development, personnel and finance. What action must each function take to achieve a target for increased return on capital? What will the organisation become if their efforts are successful? These are questions to be answered by an *action programme.*

If an action programme is to be created, all management functions need to participate. It must be ensured that the various functions collaborate together instead of planning in isolation from each other. The outcome of their collaboration must be an integrated plan defining for the whole organisation the action to be taken, the resources required and results intended.

Let us assume that a main objective of the organisation is the achievement of a higher return on capital already invested in the business, and that this cannot be achieved solely by the capital projects in the strategic plan. Thus there is a gap to be filled. The procedure is as follows:

**1** Discussions are held with the heads of the functions to decide how each of them can contribute to improve the return on capital (see Figure 1:4). This traces the links between return on capital and a number of factors wholly or partly under the control of the different management functions. It shows that all of these factors, ranging from improved labour productivity to procedures for paying suppliers have their effect on profit on capital employed. If it is part of the strategic plan to increase the return from, say, 10 per cent to 15 per cent, a worthwhile procedure is to discuss with each manager in turn what improvement (if any) he believes he can achieve in the items listed in the right hand column, looking a year or so ahead. What percentage increase in labour productivity seems possible? What improvement could be made in process efficiency by, for example, reducing fuel requirements for each unit of output?

**2** A questionnaire is designed which asks each management function to express its intentions for the future under a variety of headings. Figure 1.5 gives an example of such a questionnaire, and it will be seen that the same types of question are addressed to each of the management functions in turn. When the marketing management have answered

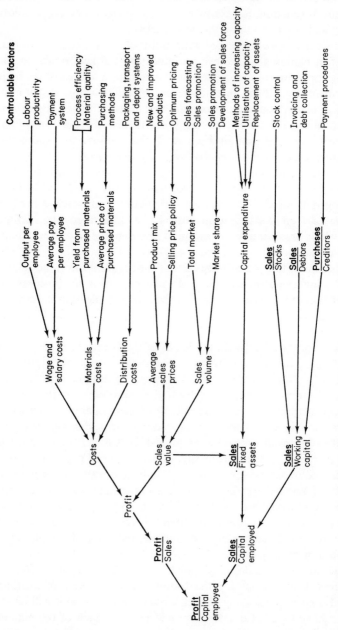

FIGURE 1:4 LINKS BETWEEN RETURN ON CAPITAL AND FACTORS INFLUENCING ITS POSSIBLE IMPROVEMENT

1    *Marketing*

(a) *Objectives*
For the following items, where do we stand now, what do we aim to achieve by 1972–3 and what might we achieve by 1977–8 ? Local Market share—Exports—New products sold—Sales Volume—Selling Prices—Revenue—Productivity of Marketing Manpower—Trading Profit as % of revenue—from existing products—from new products

(b) *Assumptions*
On what major assumptions (in regard to possible important future developments largely outside our control) is our plan based?
*Examples:*
The broad economic outlook
Growth, or otherwise, of the user industries
Changing requirements of existing customers
New types of customer and new uses we hope to supply
Effects of:
  Government policy:
    Import duties and controls and development of Free Trade Areas
    Price controls
    Regulations connected with safety, health, building standards, etc, favouring or hindering our sales
  Competition:
    From our type of product
    From other products

(c) *Policy and action proposed to achieve the objectives*
What broad policy does the plan envisage to achieve the results in (a) above? What action do we plan to take during the next five years to carry out this policy? When will this action be taken?
*Examples:*
Marketing organization
Distribution channels
Changes in the product range
Changes in the mix of products
Standardisation of product
Pricing and/or terms of payment
What action do we propose for any unprofitable products?

FIG. 1.5 QUESTIONNAIRE TO BE
CIRCULATED TO EACH MANAGEMENT FUNCTION,
INVITING EXPRESSIONS OF INTENTION FOR
THE FUTURE

(d) *Help needed*
What particular help will be needed from the rest of the company if the marketing plan is to be achieved? When?
*Examples:*
Manpower
Services—such as market research
Product development

2      *Technical*
(a) *Objectives*
What are the main technical objectives which must be achieved if the rest of this plan is to be successful? Where do we stand now, what do we aim to achieve by 1972/3, and what might we achieve by 1977/8?
*Examples:*
Improvement of existing products
Development of new products
Improvement of existing processes
Development of new processes
What are the priorities?
What is the envisaged overall annual expenditure on research and development?
(b) *Assumptions*
What assumptions have been made about competitive products and processes?
(c) *Policy and action proposed to reach the objectives*
For each technical objective, what action is proposed?

3      *Production*
(a) *Objectives*
For the following items where do we stand now, what do we aim to achieve by 1972/3, and what might we achieve by 1977/8?
Volume of output
Efficiency of plant (yields, etc)
Capacity utilisation
Efficiency of subsequent processing (losses, etc)
Efficiency of maintenance operations
Completion of major capital products
Labour productivity—all works employees
Stock to sales ratio
Unit costs
(b) *Assumptions*
On what major assumption (in regard to possible important future developments largely outside our control) is our production plan based?

FIG. 1.5 *cont.*

*Examples:*
Our technical progress in particular areas
Assumptions about competitive processes
Licensing arrangements

(c) *Policy and action proposed to achieve the objectives*
What broad policy will we follow to achieve the results in (a) above? What action do we plan to take during the next five years to carry out this policy? When will this action be taken?
*Examples:*
Construct new plant or improve existing processes?
Attack particular kinds of cost?
Concentration of production
Closure of any surplus capacity
Standardisation of product

(d) *Help needed*
What particular help will be needed from the rest of the company if the production plan is to be achieved? When?
*Examples:*
Assistance from engineering
Assistance from work study
Assistance from personnel

4    *Distribution*

(a) *Objectives*
For the following items, where do we stand now, what do we aim to achieve by 1972/3, and what might we achieve by 1977/8?
Lead-time from receipt of order to despatch
Labour productivity
Distribution costs (per foot, ton, etc.) sold
Distribution costs as % of revenue

(b) *Assumptions*
On what major assumptions (in regard to possible important future developments largely outside our control) is our plan based?
*Examples:*
Possible legislation on rail or road transport
Containerisation, palletisation, etc.,
Changing costs of alternative forms of transport
Willingness of our customers to receive in a different manner

(c) *Policy and action proposed to reach the objectives*
What broad policy will we follow to get the results in (a) above? What action do we plan to take during the next five years to carry out this policy? When will this action be taken?

FIG. 1.5. *cont.*

*Examples:*
New methods of packaging? Containerisation?
Establishment or relocation of depots?
Use alternative methods of transport?

(d) *Help needed*
What particular help will be needed from the rest of the company
if the distribution plan is to be achieved? When?

5     *Manpower*

(a) *Objectives*
For the following items, where do we stand now, what do we aim
to achieve by 1972/3, and what might be achieved by 1977/8?
Changes in total numbers employed
Labour productivity in total
Change in numbers of managers
Change in numbers of professional/graduate staff
Critical shortages which must be overcome

(b) *Assumptions*
On what major assumptions (in regard to possible important
future developments largely outside our control) is our plan
based?
*Examples:*
Organisational changes
Major changes in the composition of the labour force
Labour turnover
Ability to recruit particular kinds of people
Government legislation for social, welfare purposes

(c) *Policy and action to be taken to achieve the objectives*
What broad policy will we follow to get the results in (a) above?
What action do we plan to take during the next five years to carry
out this policy? When will this action be taken?
*Examples:*
To deal with any overmanning?
To obtain future management needs?
To deal with any critical shortages?

(d) *Help needed*
What particular help will be needed from the rest of the company
if the manpower plan is to be achieved?
*Examples:*
What recruitment, if any, will be needed?
What particular training needs can be identified?

FIG. 1.5 *cont.*

6 *Financial*

(a) *Objectives*
For the following items, where do we stand now, what do we aim to achieve by 1972/3, and what might we achieve by 1977/8?
Return on Sales
Turnover of capital
Return on investiment
Cash flow
Dividends

(b) *Assumptions*
On what major assumptions (in regard to possible important developments largely outside our control) is our financial plan based?
*Examples:*
Rates of inflation in respect of wages and salaries, raw materials, fuels, new plant and buildings
Foreign exchange rates and controls
Tax rates
Government financial incentives

(c) *Policy and action planned to achieve the objectives*
What management policies described earlier in the plan are considered the most important in achieving the objective for return on investment? What action do we propose to take during the next five years?
*Examples:*
Financing
Loan repayments
Dividend payments

FIG. 1.5 *cont.*

the questions in section 1, their replies are passed to technical management who answer the questions in section 2, whereupon all the answers so far accumulated are passed to production management and so on.

**3** A step-by-step list of headings is devised under which the quantitative data will be supplied which will show the results of the action programmes proposed. The form of sales forecast agreed with marketing management must provide the essential statistical data for the production plan. The headings for the quantitative data in production management's plan must ensure that the essential figures needed by distribution management are supplied. Eventually, agreement will be reached with the accountants on the form of the data which will be shown in their planned profit and loss account and balance sheet. This of course will show all the managers whether or not their joint planning will achieve the original objective for improving return on capital.

Figure 1:6 gives an example of some of the quantitative data which may be found essential. This is only a summary of headings for which figures will need to be collected. Each heading needs to be translated into the particular product names, process descriptions and so forth used in the organisation, with the various lines of figures laid out downwards on the page so that the calculations are done in the right sequence. It may be found necessary to include one or two hundred lines of figures in the complete document to make sure that the essential statistics needed are provided.

The timing of this phase of the company's planning work is complicated by the fact that it must be sequential, with marketing department starting off, followed by technical and production planning and so on, until the accountants finally convert all the previous figures to monetary terms. One management function cannot begin work on its section until another has finished on theirs. The total amount of time required by all the management functions to answer the questionnaire and complete the tables of statistical information may run into as much as two or three months or even more depending on size and complexity.

By the time the combined effort is completed, the marketing department may argue that new facts and trends have come to light which invalidate their previous sales forecasts, and thus all the related statistics contributed by other departments. There is a danger therefore that the statistical statement of the action programme will never be regarded as correct. One way of avoiding this problem is to keep to the bare minimum the amount of quantitative information asked for. Another is to

| | |
|---|---|
| (a) **Marketing** | The overall market volume (forecast) <br> Our intended share <br> Our sales volume <br> Product mix <br> Sales prices <br> Revenue <br> Marketing manpower and expenses <br> Measurements of productivity <br> Contribution to profit |
| (b) **Production** | Volume of output required <br> Yields and losses <br> Capacity required <br> % utilization of capacity <br> Additions to production facilities <br> Materials, fuel and manpower required <br> Production costs <br> Measurements of productivity <br> Contribution to profit |
| (c) **Technical** | Planned improvements in production efficiencies <br> —throughput rates <br> —yields <br> —qualities |
| (d) **Distribution** | Volumes to be shipped by alternative methods <br> Distribution facilities required <br> Manpower required <br> Distribution costs <br> Measurement of productivity <br> Contribution to profit |
| (e) **Administration** (including headquarters departments) | Timetable for services to be developed <br> Manpower <br> Expenditure <br> Measurements of productivity <br> Contribution to profit |
| (f) **Manpower** | Overall manpower strength <br> Overall productivity measurements <br> Management requirements |
| (g) **Financial results** | Sales values <br> Costs <br> Profits and profit margins <br> Capital employed <br> Sales and profits on capital employed <br> Cash flow |

FIGURE 1:6  SUMMARY OF QUANTITATIVE
DATA REQUIRED TO SHOW THE RESULTS OF
THE ACTION PROGRAMMES PROPOSED

make use of the company's computer, if there is one. This can be programmed to perform all the routine calculations required, using the statistical forecasts which can be obtained only from the managers themselves. The computer can handle alternative forecasts and thus show the management what the financial results would be if different actions were taken, such as improving labour and production efficiencies at different rates. Further it allows the consideration of alternatives to continue past the strategic phase into the action phases.

How often management should be asked to participate in creating an action programme will vary not only from one organisation to another but also between companies within a group. It is wrong to assume that they should always be prepared annually. If major decisions asked for by the strategic plan are pending and these could dramatically change the business, it is pointless to ask for preparation of action programmes until the decisions are known. Equally, if the organisation exists in a quiet environment where there is little change from year to year, it may be superfluous to ask for a new action programme each year.

## 1:7   Implementation, target setting and review

Until action programmes are agreed and the agreement is communicated to the management, they cannot be implemented. So a procedure has to be worked out whereby agreement is clearly obtained. The statements and calculations prepared by the various functions have to be collated and checked for gaps and inconsistency and to ensure that the final document gives a balanced overall picture for consideration by the board.

Formal presentation of the action plan to the board in the presence of the most senior functional managers is a valuable means of communication. It gives an opportunity to explain the thinking behind the proposed courses of action, and the board in turn can question any aspect it wishes. If the board gives only perfunctory attention to the document, and there is little or no discussion, this will suggest that the planning efforts have partly failed.

What is required from the board is either their clear agreement to the preferred courses of action and action programmes proposed by the main management functions, or else a clear statement of any alternative courses of action which the board prefers. It is worth making a considerable effort to get this clearly stated and equally clearly communicated back to the management functions. Otherwise managers may complain that their plans are never agreed and that their efforts have been a waste of time.

The action programme finally agreed by the board might easily be left to gather dust in a filing cabinet. How is this to be prevented? How can it be ensured that action is taken as a result of the hard thinking which has been done and agreed? An answer lies in the adoption of *management by objectives*, which is a management practice aimed at integrating the efforts of all managers with the overall objectives of the organisation. Figure 1:7 summarises very broadly part of the sequence of events involved.

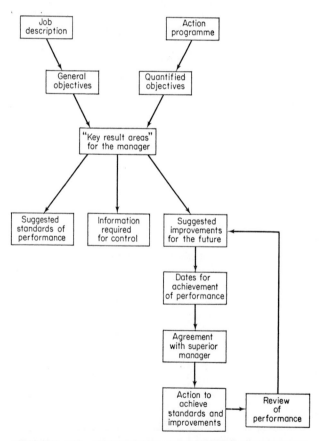

FIGURE 1:7   SEQUENCE OF EVENTS INVOLVED IN IMPLEMENTING THE ACTION PROGRAMME

In a typical situation a works manager, for example, holds a meeting with the managers of his factory to explain the action plan which has been agreed for his works. This may define quantified improvements which are desired in several areas; such as lead time from receipt of order to despatch, increased throughput rates, larger output yields from a given input, reduction of defects, reduced labour turnover, and reduction of surplus stocks. Each manager in the works is asked to consider what he personally can do to help achieve these improvements.

At this point it is valuable if each manager possesses a job description which defines the general objectives of the job (regardless of the particular individual who happens to occupy the job at any one moment) and also the reporting relationships above and below. An example of the general objectives of a personnel manager is given in Figure 1:8.

---

**Job title:**               PERSONNEL MANAGER

**Responsible to:**      WORKS MANAGER

**Responsible to him:**  Personnel officer
                          Safety officer
                          Training officer
                          Welfare officer
                          Senior policeman

**General objectives**

1   To promote and maintain good industrial relations

2   To recruit staff and hourly-paid employees of the required number and quality to maintain efficient establishments

3   To ensure implementation of company agreements and policies in respect of wages, salaries and conditions of employment

4   To ensure implementation of company welfare standards throughout the works and to help rehabilitate sick and injured employees

5   To identify what training is needed by all employees and to ensure that the required training is organised

6   To minimise accidents within the works by ensuring safe and healthy working conditions and compliance with the Factories Act

7   To administer works security, in liaison with the company security officer

---

FIGURE 1:8  EXAMPLE OF JOB DESCRIPTION
Showing the general objectives of a personnel manager

From these general objectives and also from any quantified objectives defined by the works manager, the personnel manager then defines for himself his *key result areas*, or the most important results which he feels he should aim to achieve. In the example attached (Figure 1:9) the personnel manager has chosen "Employment" and "Training" as his first two key areas. Under the heading of "Employment" he has included as a key task the reduction of labour turnover, which was one of the objectives notified by the works manager as part of the overall action programme. Within this particular task the personnel manager goes on to define what he regards as a reasonable standard of performance now, what information he has for measuring his performance, and what improvement he feels he can achieve. The reduction of labour turnover by 5 per cent which he has proposed will have a target date attached to it which might be three or four months away. These suggested standards and improvements are then taken by the personnel manager to the works manager for agreement.

To assemble their ideas in this way is neither easy nor rapid for most managers. They will almost certainly need the aid of a specialist adviser who has experience of management by objectives and it will be found that up to six or eight hours, or sometimes more, is normally needed by most managers to clarify their own thinking. The adviser will probably accompany him to the meeting at which the chief executive's agreement is then sought. If the manager's thinking has been carefully done it will generally be found that 80 to 90 per cent of the subordinate's proposals are accepted as being in line with the action programme laid down for the works or other management function involved. Once accepted, these standards and improvements can be incorporated in financial budgets for each of the departments.

Each manager is then expected to do his best to achieve the improvements which have been agreed and to report back for a formal review of progress at some agreed future date, perhaps three, six, nine or twelve months later. The opportunity is then taken to examine the reasons for any failure to achieve the agreed improvements, to agree on any necessary action and to develop a revised list of improvements for the next few months. Again, the presence of the specialist adviser is desirable at least at the first of these performance reviews so as to ensure that it takes place and is effective. Keeping up the impetus thereafter is a major responsibility of the adviser.

In an organisation with not more than about forty managers it may be possible for one person to take on responsibility for introducing the procedures for management by objectives during a year. In very large

| | KEY AREAS | ACCEPTABLE STANDARD OF PERFORMANCE |
|---|---|---|
| 1 | EMPLOYMENT<br>(a) To supply the number and quality of personnel as requisitioned by managers at minimum recruitment cost | (i) Only 5 % of vacancies are outstanding for more than one month<br>(ii) Follow up reports are 90 % satisfactory<br>(iii) Recruitment costs average not more than £100 per recruit |
| | (b) To reduce labour turnover | Labour turnover to be kept below 20 % annually for males and 30 % for females |
| 2 | TRAINING<br>To make the company training schemes satisfy local and group requirements | (i) Departmental managers needs for trainees are established at least annually<br>(ii) All trainees have a laid down training programme<br>(iii) 90 % of trainees complete their training successfully |

FIG. 1.9

organisations with hundreds of managers a choice has to be made whether to attempt to introduce management by objectives throughout the organisation over a relatively brief period such as two or three years, or whether to spread the process over five to ten years. The first alternative is superficially attractive but may demand a team of at least ten specialist advisers who are difficult to recruit externally. They

| INFORMATION AVAILABLE TO MEASURE PERFORMANCE | SUGGESTED IMPROVEMENTS |
|---|---|
| Personnel department vacancy list and monthly return | No suggestion made |
| No control document exists | Introduce a system to ascertain after one month the suitability of new employees for continued service |
| No control document exists | Get a monthly report on recruitment costs from accounts department |
| Monthly departmental labour turnover record | Reduce labour turnover by 5% by introducing and controlling an improved works induction procedure and by keeping earnings in line with those offered in the area |
| List of Managers needs for trainees kept in personnel department | |
| ⎰ Half yearly reports on each trainee's<br>⎱ progress at college and in the<br>⎰ works by the supervisor and<br>⎱ departmental manager | Much closer contact is needed with the departmental managers and trainees to ensure that trainees are adhering to a laid down programme and that they are progressing satisfactorily at all times. For this purpose a full-time training officer should be appointed |

FIGURE 1:9   EXTRACT FROM LISTING OF KEY
AREAS
Showing those tasks the personnel manager considers to be
his most important objectives

will probably have to be found from among the most able existing managers and then trained. The slower programme may be started quite adequately with only two or three specialists who can be assigned to selected parts of the organisation where the concept of management by objectives has the strongest support and thus the greatest possibility of success.

Unfortunately, a very slow introduction of management by objectives will deprive the organisation of an essential link between the action plan and its implementation by management generally. In these circumstances the organisation will probably have to rely on financial budgets only for control purposes.

Acknowledgement is made to the journal "Long Range Planning" for permission to reprint the tables on pages 13 and 19.

―――――――――――― *TWO* ――――――――――――

# Market Planning

*by Hugh Buckner*

Corporate success can stem from many aspects of business operation. In some cases, such as selling washing powders to the housewife, it is high pressure merchandising that is the key to successful operations. In others, such as marketing chemical formulations it is the solid reputation that comes from consistently successful technical problem solving. In further activities such as vehicle leasing, the key area is the painstaking attention to detailed costs, both present and future, in a business with established sales prices. To be useful, planning needs to focus on the function or combination of functions which makes or breaks the operation in that business. Market planning is not, therefore, the main component of all companies' plans, although it will certainly be so for many companies.

### 2:1   Market planning and forecasting

It is fashionable to be market oriented, which simply means that all activities in the business are directed toward customer satisfaction. The marketing concept does not mean that those with the marketing title are necessarily the most important in achieving this end. For example, in markets where the main customer need is for innovation, a marketing-oriented corporate plan would need to start from the research and development plan.

This is the starting place for market planning. Firms, once converted to formal planning, see that the natural first step is the estimate of sales ahead. The second step is often a detailed consideration of what the customer wants. This has in many cases led to an over-emphasis on the market plan in terms of the other components, which tend to be seen as subordinate. There is then an obvious risk of failure because the plan is not realistic, or the company as a whole is not committed to it. Where the marketing function does not determine success in a business, the other activities concerned must play a major role in helping the market plan to unfold. Thus, market planning is vitally different from sales programming. The market plan refers to the way in which the company is to relate to its markets and all those in a company who are in charge of activities which are vital to success must play a part in its production. Indeed, as with corporate planning as a whole, most of the gain will be from the interaction and unity of ideas that takes place as the market plan is formed.

A market plan is not a forecast. Ideally it is a course of action for today designed to place the company in the best position to take advantage of whatever may happen tomorrow. It follows from this that market plans are made for action *today*. If no action is needed today then plans should be reconstructed at a later date. In reaching planning decisions *forecasts* are needed. Operational (tactical) forecasts should extend forward as far as it is believable to project the data. This is seldom longer than one or two years and is often shorter. Environmental (strategic) forecasts need to operate between the "believable accuracy" of operational forecasts and the dates needed for planning changes in resource allocations. Operational forecasts cover such items as stocks, product ranges and sales levels. Environmental forecasts cover user needs, market areas and growth forces. Thus, normally, operations plans extend for one year and strategic for five years in detail. Textile companies in fashion businesses need shorter periods and energy companies or corporations need longer.

Definitions are confused in the forecasting area. Some talk of environmental factors being those which affect the company but over which the the company has no control—other than strategically in choosing to compete in that business at all. In this sense environmental factors are variables which may be close to the company such as the number of competitors. However, environmental analysis usually refers to the study of the larger scale, slower changing forces surrounding the company. These may be technological, economic, governmental and so on. The company can affect these, but only to a small extent because of their size. In this sense market analysis would be the term to apply to the study of the close to home factors and environmental analysis to those farther away.

In developing forecasts, the essential from a strategy point of view is to isolate the areas where a change could produce a dramatic effect. These are the aspects with which a company can work to alter the trends.

In every market and also in the features and technology of the products that supply it there is a small number of crucial factors. These are not the same in the alternative ways of serving the market. Some of these crucial factors are in the control of the company (such as types of distribution adopted) and others clearly are not (such as hire purchase restrictions). Naturally the strategy which has most of the crucial factors under the company's control has a good deal to commend it. One way of identifying crucial factors is to locate those points where an error would place the company seriously at risk. For example, in some markets, taking the right decisions about the distribution structure would be far more important than determining the right price. In other markets a careful selection of the positions of products in a range when compared with those of the competitor would be crucial. Managers should not accept a forecast without these crucial factors being identified and the form of action needed to vary the factor indicated.

## 2:2  A system for market planning

Figure 2:1 shows a system for market planning. It starts with five major inputs and moves through a series of analysis stages until finally action plans and the schedules to achieve them are drawn up. It can be seen that there is a firm separation maintained between the future of the products already in service and those which are expected to follow. The former, called the *momentum line* is an expression of what will happen if the present operations continue as they are now. Thus the momentum line includes those products already sold on the market and already committed replacements or developments of existing products and services. The momentum line does not include new products, new markets or the expected results of research and development. These latter developments should be analysed and reported separately. The reason for this firm separation is twofold:

**1**  The forecasts of existing product sales should be of a higher order of accuracy than those of new products. There is often little basis for the sales estimates of new products. It would be asking too much of a manager whose product group was not performing well not to inflate his estimates of new product sales with a little hope. If the forecasts

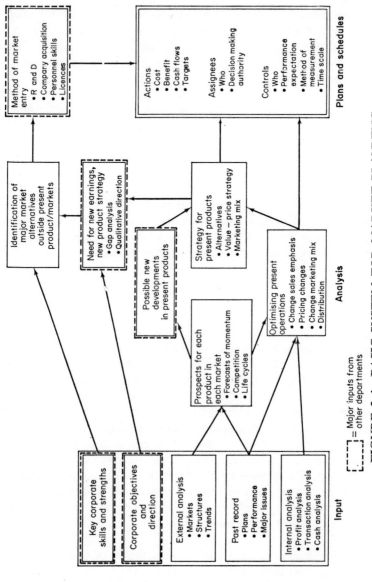

FIGURE 2:1  BASIC SYSTEM FOR MARKET PLANNING

are separate it can be clearly seen how much of future sales are from which source.

2 Until the plan is formulated the company is not committed to introducing the new products. If it is found that the company's market penetration can be optimised by concentrating development in one area then developments in others may be dropped. It is dangerously restricting the search for alternatives to mix the two types of forecasts.

## 2:3 Areas of internal analysis

The internal analysis revolves around the basic organisation and resources of the company to show the reasons for past sales and profit and to identify areas where forecasts and actions need to be modified for internal factors. The major areas to be considered are:

1 Past and current product (market performance, market size and structure, market share, user needs and buying practices, competition, requirements for successful operation).

2 Possible new projects (objective, expected sales levels, potable profit levels, risk, uniqueness or proprietary aspects).

3 Sales records (sales contracts, sales records to major customers, price history).

4 Marketing management (age, education, training, experience, record).

5 Financial results (profit/loss by product line and customer groups, profit/loss account, balance sheet).

6 Company organisation and management style (formal, informal, functional, product group, geographical).

7 Forms of corporate control (committees, records, performance ratings, forecasts, budgets, capital expenditure controls).

8 Production (machinery, processes, key controls).

9 Plant and facilities (owned, rented).

It is important for those marketing a company's products to know which are profitable and at what range mix and so on. Yet surprisingly often market plans are formulated without this information, often because the companies concerned do not have it themselves. Accountants are often reluctant to produce figures for profitability by product line because it involves judgement decisions on allocating overheads.

## 2:4   Determining profit by product line

The importance of determing profit by product line can be seen in
Table 2:1, which shows the present sales of a light engineering company
having five main product lines. It also shows the contribution being
made by each product after charging the direct costs. It can be seen

|  | SALES | CONTRIBUTION | | ESTIMATED PROFIT | |
|---|---|---|---|---|---|
|  | £ | £ | % | £ | % |
| Product A | 160 000 | 35 000 | 22 | 25 000 | 15.6 |
| Product B | 60 000 | 40 000 | 66 | 25 000 | 41.5 |
| Product C | 212 000 | 64 000 | 30 | 20 000 | 10.0 |
| Product D | 55 000 | 16 000 | 29 | 5 000 | 9.0 |
| Product E | 179 000 | 54 000 | 30 | (6 000) | (3.3) |
| Others | 84 000 | 25 000 | 30 | 1 000 | 1.0 |
| TOTAL | 750 000 | 234 000 | 31 | 70 000 | 9.0 |

TABLE 2.1   CONTRIBUTION AND ESTIMATED
ACTUAL PROFIT BY PRODUCT LINE
( ) = loss

that product A is substandard on a contribution basis, yielding only
22 per cent against a company average of 31 per cent. However, if all
costs are allocated, product A emerges as well above company average
with a profit of 16 per cent compared with a company average of 9 per
cent. The reason is simply that product A is mainly a factored item
requiring little work by the company. Thus, while it had a low contribution to group overheads, it is not making use of the services they
provide.

In contrast, product E was satisfactory on contribution but because of
its awkwardness in handling and the large number of small transactions
involved it was actually loss making. This is a typical case. All companies over a period of time tend to manufacture products which "fit"
their factory. Thus, there is a built in tendency to favour a high contribution rather than a high profit.

Figure 2:2 shows the figures in Table 2:1 pictorially. To many people
figures do not mean a great deal and while much discussion will follow
the presentation of a table it is quite clear in Figure 2:2 that products A,
B and C dominate the others in terms of profit. Similarly, in the lower
chart the brutal fact emerges that all work on product E simply loses

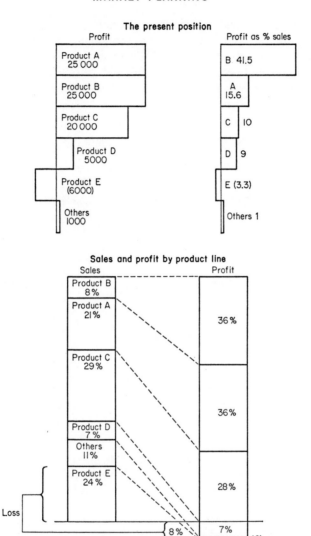

FIGURE 2:2   GRAPHIC REPRESENTATION OF
MOMENTUM LINE PROJECTIONS SHOWN IN
TABLE 2:2

the company what it made on product *D* and the "others" category.

To accomplish the profit analysis all costs have to be allocated to the products. Direct costs, providing they are collected in a meaningful way, are no problem, but the allocation of indirect costs can cause the most amazing and irrational behaviour on the part of managements. "Pet" products are allocated few overhead costs; claims are made that the present situation is not normal; statistics are produced to show the change that would occur if product *E* could only sell above a certain amount, with the strong implication that it is the marketing men's fault it has not, and so on.

## 2:5   Dealing with the unprofitable product

The realisation is growing that accounting is an inexact science and perhaps managements will be increasingly willing to commit their judgement as to product profit to paper. The importance of this analysis to a marketing plan can be seen in Table 2:2. Product *A* has the greatest prospects for expansion. Product *C* is expected to decline and the modest

|  | SALES | | PROFIT | |
|---|---|---|---|---|
|  | 1969/70 £ | 1973/74 £ | 1969/70 £ | 1973/74 £ |
| Product *A* | 160 000 | 291 000 | 25 000 | 62 000 |
| Product *B* | 60 000 | 79 000 | 25 000 | 47 000 |
| Product *C* | 212 000 | 250 000 | 20 000 | 30 000 |
| Product *D* | 55 000 | 40 000 | 5 000 | (1 000) |
| Product *E* | 179 000 | 200 000 | (6 000) | (7 000) |
| Others | 84 000 | 90 000 | 1 000 | 1 000 |
| TOTAL | 750 000 | 950 000 | 70 000 | 132 000 |

TABLE 2:2   MOMENTUM LINE PROJECTIONS
Present sales and profits projected from market estimates assuming no basic changes in or additions to the business
( ) = loss

growth expected in product *E* will simply make it even less profitable. Before a market plan can be constructed the impact of these factors needs discussion among all decision makers.

The above is not to suggest that unprofitable products should automatically be divested. Market studies may show ways in which profitability can be improved through a creative approach. However successful, businessmen can be observed to differ here. Many would feel that the effort spent in turning round a loss making product line would be better spent in making the successful products more successful. The decision will depend on the extent of opportunity facing the company in all its markets. Of course, unprofitable products in declining markets will be terminated.

The fixed costs associated with a product to be terminated cannot always be eliminated in the short term and the timing of its run down naturally needs integration with other departments. The following is an outline checklist for unprofitable products:

1    Is the market potential worth the effort?
2    Could the effort be better spent on other products?
3    Is the product group recently launched?
 (a)  Higher than expected launching costs
 (b)  When is it expected to be profitable?
 (c)  Controls to ensure it is on target?
4    Can prices be raised?
 (a)  Selective?
 (b)  Total?
5    Can production costs be reduced (with cheaper components for example)?
6    Have possible reasons for internal inefficiency been examined?
7    What would be the effect on profitability of reducing marketing effort on this product (either total or altering marketing mix)?
8    Is range width or depth excessive?
9    Can small buyers be eliminated (or minimum order charge introduced)?
10    What is profitability, by customer group or type?
11    If the product group is eliminated, what happens to fixed costs?
12    Is the product group substantially independent of others?
13    Could the product group be profitable in another environment (is it saleable)?

In addition to profit by product line, profit analysis should be carried out for other factors. For consumer goods companies, sales territory analysis is important. For service companies, or those selling in large numbers of small orders, the analysis needs to be carried out by end market and by account size and so on. Figure 2:3 shows an analysis of sales and profits in groups of return on sales for a company undertaking jobbing operations. Once the jobs were sorted in this way the

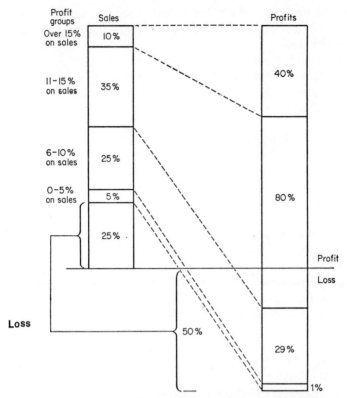

FIGURE 2:3  ANALYSIS OF SALES AND PROFIT BY
PROFITABILITY GROUPS FOR A COMPANY
UNDERTAKING JOBBING OPERATIONS

relationships and therefore the implications for market action among
the loss makers became apparent.

## 2:6  Identifying the key factors

The second major area of internal analysis for the market plan involves
the identification of "levers" which can be used to increase output per
unit cost. Almost always these revolve around a concentration of effort
on certain key areas. The simple fact that a small number of actions
produce most of the results in all business activities is not applied in
marketing as widely as commonsense would lead one to believe. Figure
2:4 illustrates that probably some 80 per cent of results in marketing

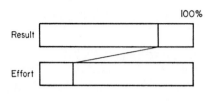

This rule however is built into most situations

• Customers do not want 100% solutions:
you have to identify whether 80, 85,
90, 95 percent is needed

• Customers will not pay 80% for an 80%
solution. They will only pay 30-40%.
Your problem is: Can you detect the 20%
area to put your effort

Real situation

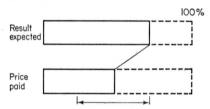

FIGURE 2:4   THE 80–20 RULE
This implies that probably some 80 per cent of results in
marketing are achieved by 20 per cent effort

are achieved by 20 per cent of effort. In practice, difficulties in recognising the key factors on which to concentrate leads to perhaps 20 to 40 per cent of effort being needed to produce 80 per cent of results. However, one point is vital. Almost never should a company undertake to produce a 100 per cent result in any aspect of its marketing. Those who produce 100 per cent solutions after spending 100 per cent of effort are not competing in the real world. In most markets the workings of this rule have already had effect. In these cases an 80 per cent result is required (in, say, product life to first failure, or efficiency of fuel usage, or response to service calls) and the market is prepared to pay (say) 60 per cent. Obviously those rushing in without considering the 80–20 rule will produce the result at about 70 to 80 per cent of the cost and they will have low profits. Those who can identify more closely the key issues and act accordingly will increase their profits.

Despite the obvious truth of the above rule that concentration of effort is the key to productivity, marketing men most often follow other social rules:

**1** Marketing men, advertising specialists, and so on have formed associations which develop standards of one form or another. While these bodies raise technical standards, their effect on creativity and individualism is often crushing. The resulting uniformity of approach can be seen in all companies.

**2** Many specialists indulge excessively in problem solving for its own sake. The higher qualified the individual the more this is evident. With the growing complexity of marketing and technology more decisions are made by highly qualified specialists who often have not had the hard experience or the incentive to cut through problems without solving them.

**3** Company development is often subordinated to personal development in terms of published work. The individual produces ideal solutions to problems that should have been amputated before they required any effort to solve.

The above does not include inefficiency or lack of knowledge and intelligence, all of which add to the list. In examining their present operations, marketing men need to note how far towards a 100 per cent job is needed in each area and where the 20 per cent of effort needed to achieve it is likely to lie.

### 2:7   Analysis of major costs

The third area of internal analysis is a close examination of the major costs. These are as follows:

1    *Marketing mix:*
  (*a*)  Advertising
  (*b*)  Promotion
  (*c*)  Samples
  (*d*)  Personnel
2    *Sales force:*
  (*a*)  Premises
  (*b*)  Personnel
  (*c*)  Vehicles
3    *Market research:*
  (*a*)  Fees
  (*b*)  Personnel

4  *Services:*
 (*a*) Application engineering
 (*b*) Prototype development
 (*c*) Others
5  *Distribution:*
 (*a*) Depots
 (*b*) Vehicles
 (*c*) Fuel
 (*d*) Personnel
6  *Stocks of finished products*
7  *Sales and marketing overhead*
8  *Discounts, rebates*
9  *Credit bad debts*
10  *Bad goods*
11  *Lost sales:*
 (*a*) Out of stock
 (*b*) Others
12  *Emergency costs*

In conducting this analysis, the aim is to discover the reasons why each cost is at its specific level. Primarily, at this stage, it is inefficiency that is being located. Wherever possible a run back of each cost over three years (five years if available) should be studied and reasons for changes evaluated against expected and actual results. Sometimes reorganisations, mergers and major changes make previous figures obsolete or the figures may not be recorded in a usable form. Then commonsense has to be used.

The first seven major headings refer to physical costs. They should all be identifiable and have a specific reason why they were set at the levels concerned and why one was used in preference to the other (for example, direct sales as opposed to advertising or direct mail, or numbers of salesmen in specific territories). Headings 8, 9 and 10 are also cost of sale items and need careful evaluation. Headings 11 and 12 can only be estimated from the frequency and the type of operation which has to be mounted to retrieve the situation.

The results of the internal analysis should be a clear understanding of:

1    The sales mix of products which makes for maximum profit and the separate mix which makes for maximum contribution

2    Likely problems and time scales needed to bring overhead structure in line with the maximum profit earners
3    That percentage of a total solution which is being provided by each product at what percentage of total cost
4    Major marketing costs and their reasons

## 2:8   Constructing environmental forecasts

The initial step in examining the position in the market of the company's present products is to study the environment for the company as a whole. Only following this are separate forecasts made for individual products. This ensures that the various product forecasts are based on the same assumptions. The environmental research isolates broad trends that indicate the areas within which the most exploitable opportunities are likely to occur. The scope of the environmental analysis depends on the company concerned. A small company may need to look little further than the outlook for its specific end user industries. That is, a company solely supplying doors to the building industry may look little further than the forecasts of housing demand. A large, diversified company may need to cover a significant area of the national economy.

Much of the data needed for the construction of an environmental forecast is available from published sources. All forecasts are of course based on assumptions. A forecast is a statement of the expected change in some variable such as product sales or profit level against the background of other factors which are assumed to be fixed—constant prices, government policy, or entry to the common market. The likelihood of each of these assumptions needs to be questioned and if necessary alternative forecasts prepared. When few factors are regarded as fixed, a family of forecasts needs to be assembled to cover the alternative circumstances. Several of these alternatives, while separate and different, will probably call for the same actions on the part of the company. In these cases the soundest course is the one designed to meet the group of alternatives needing the same action and possessing the highest combined probability of occurring.

The extent to which forecasting is an art is often a shock to those not normally involved in marketing. So much depends on qualitative factors such as images, fashions and attitudes among buyers as to who is or is not good. These are by no means confined to consumer markets. All forecasts need to rely heavily on market and business understanding and complex non-mathematical jumps from one set of figures to another in order to incorporate qualitative data. Models of markets help significantly in this area but for most companies having a wide range of products sold to a number of end markets the costs in market modelling are as yet prohibitive and the number of variables to be considered vast.

The choice of the items to forecast is vital to accuracy. "No forecast can look further ahead than is believable. Certain items in an economy are patently slow to change and may be known up to ten years or more in advance. Age groups, family size, income growth and distribution and the learned skills of a population are obvious examples. So are the basic problems that a society faces, such as shortage of skilled labour and resources or a difficulty in applying modern technology. These problems lead directly to growth forces—towards labour saving equipment for example—and all economic change derives from these slowly changing forces." [Hugh Buckner, "Formulae for Forecasting Management Today," *Annual Review of Management Techniques*, 1968.] The environmental study should concentrate on growth forces. Figure 2:5 shows some examples. These can be thought of as escalators going upwards. It is far easier to reach the top on an up escalator than on a down one, no matter how hard you run. However many of the ingredients for success a company's product has in itself, the more growth forces support the technology, the customers and the whole surrounding environment the better.

## 2:9 Assessing maturity of existing products

An important function of external analysis is for the company to build a good appreciation of where its products are on their life cycle. Figure 2:6 shows the market life cycle. A company will have some products—future earners—which are in the early stages of development. Sales will be small and there will be initial losses.

Other products—today's earners—will be in the growth stage. Sales will be increasing and profit levels will be good. Other products—yesterday's earners—will be mature and competition will have reduced profit levels. There is no way a company can determine the prospects ahead for its products from information inside the company. Tempting as it is to project the product's past record of sales into the future it is also the one way to nullify the whole planning procedure. Only the users can state their plans for future uptake, their requirements in terms of technical specification and their reasons for changing preferences for this or that competitor. Of course the data that can be obtained from customers by internal means should be used. Salesmen's reports,

| | CONSUMER | COMMERCIAL | INSTITUTIONAL | INDUSTRIAL |
|---|---|---|---|---|
| **Basic growth forces** | Population growth and changes<br>Increased leisure time<br>Increased discretionary income<br>Higher educational level | Labour saving and cost reduction<br>Higher performance standards<br>Need for faster and better records<br>Need for more and faster communications<br>Increasing complexity of business | Labour saving<br>Higher health and educational standards<br>Population growth and changes<br>Increased discretionary income | Labour saving<br>Lower cost materials and processes<br>Better appearances and quality<br>Defence requirements<br>Research and development<br>Capital conservation |
| **Major markets**<br>**Principal growth areas** | Personal care and health<br>Home operations<br>Personal finance<br>Leisure, education, culture, travel | Labour saving products<br>Information collection and utilization<br>Leasing<br>Merchandising<br>Newer transportation<br>Business for employee well-being | Medical and dental<br>Education<br>Institutional building | Chemical products and synthetic materials<br>Automation—electronics, instrumentation and control<br>Energy generation and distribution<br>Water and effluent treatment<br>Research and development<br>Leasing |

FIGURE 2:5  BASIC GROWTH FORCES THAT CREATE PRODUCT OPPORTUNITIES

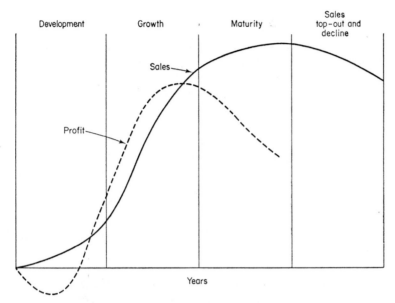

FIGURE 2:6   THE MARKET LIFE CYCLE
Illustrating that many products build up gradually to peak
sales and profit and then level out or decline

guarantee cards, complaints and the past record of sales are all indicative
and can be used to reduce the amount of field work needed.

Most of the information will however be obtained from users through
personnel interviews. These would normally be unstructured and require
some degree of skill on the part of those conducting the interview. The
interviewers probe the user's needs in detail and get behind respondents'
statements to evaluate real needs. Answers from respondents such as
"we could do with that to solve some process control problems we have"
need to be probed until they become "we have heating problems in oil
which cause phase changes and wedging rather than layering of the
liquid. As a result we get an uneven end product. I estimate this costs
us £250 000 a year."

Only by constantly collecting information in depth can a reliable
picture of market demand be constructed. It need hardly be emphasised
that if this process is by-passed or other than comprehensive, confidence
cannot be placed in the outcome. The process should either be conducted
in full or the company should realise that it is planning intuitively.

## 2:10   Assessing the market share

Once developed, the company's market forecasts and the expected results of corporate action on those forecasts can be rationalised and the two-part transition from market forecast to sales forecast and sales forecast to profit forecast is made. In projecting market share there are few really meaningful guidelines that are generally applicable. Small improvements in an established market share are reasonably easy to predict. For example an alteration in sales territories would probably have an easily estimated effect on market share.

Forecasting the market share which can be obtained in a new market is more complex. Normally up to about a ten per cent share of a new market can be realised without causing major competitor reactions. After this the likely competitor moves need to be considered—all will tend to reduce the market share that could otherwise be achieved and some will also reduce profit margins.

In the market with many competitors and where the top three do not hold more than (say) 60 per cent of the market, the third largest market share should be reasonably attainable. Where a single company holds an established and dominant market share, there being no significant other competition, a market share of some 15–20 per cent should be attainable with a product that is genuinely exploiting areas of dissatisfaction.

Share changes in markets where three or four companies together hold some 80 per cent are more difficult to achieve. To differ significantly from the above, a company needs to have sound reasons why its offering is really better than that of the competitors. Products similar in important characteristics to competitor products sold in approximately the same way are not sufficient. Any major deviation from established practices is a risk which can work in both directions.

Once the share is estimated, the profit projection is determined by using the present percentage return on sales modified to include:

1    Profits from increased volume
2    Leverage due to increased volume
3    Improvements in efficiency
4    Improvements in product/profit mix
5    Improvements in transaction mix

## 2:11   Factors affecting profit contribution

To determine the future profit contribution of each product in its separate markets the data needed falls into the following areas:

1   Market size and main product breakdowns
2   Market structure, major commercial characteristics, and key user requirements
3   Future market, projections of commercial and technological factors
4   User industry requirements and buying practices
5   Analysis of competitive strengths
6   Determination of the requirements for successful operation

When examining user industry requirements, special attention should be given to the needs for product range width and depth. Customers may demand an extensive range width. That is, they need a number of related product groups such as pumps, motors and valves from the same manufacturers. Equally, users may demand a large range depth. That is, the number of products in a group, such as pumps of different capacities and so on.

Determining whether the range width and depth are correct is a matter of balancing opposing requirements. A wider range provides salesmen with more sales a call but reduces the concentration of the salesmen. Similarly, a deeper range is always of advantage to users but causes smaller production runs than would be possible with a shallower range. The acid question is: did the most recent additions to width and depth add significantly to total profits?

In some businesses the problem of range width is more concerned with combating seasonal and trade cycles in one or more of the products. The search for anticyclical products is an attractive idea but usually very difficult in practice. The real answer for most companies is to keep a high proportion of costs variable and use the flexibility to maintain a good utilisation.

## 2:12   Need for alternatives

The key to successful corporate decisions is the extent of the range of alternatives from which the decision is taken. The simplicity of this rule is deceptive, however, and many managers find thinking of alternatives almost impossible. The basic reasons are:

1    *Tunnel vision.* The operation has been performed in such
     and such a way for so long that alternatives just cannot be
     imagined
2    *Fault-finding.* People automatically think of reasons why a
     new solution would not work before the solution has been
     fully thought through
3    *N.I.H.* (*not invented here*). Other department's (or just
     other person's) thoughts and experience are often needed
     to think through a new solution. These persons may not
     be prepared to be helpful
4    *Product orientation.* Overconcentration on cost-cutting,
     efficiency, existing technical performance improvement,
     and so on, at the expense of value considerations to the
     user

Creativity demands a willingness not just to make new marketing
decisions and policies but also to reconsider old ones. Many past decisions were made in the absence of the further facts which have since
unfolded. To be able to generate alternatives may need a willingness
to restructure old decisions. This is not meant to imply the daily retaking
of the same decisions but simply that in the key areas of marketing (the
20 per cent that count), marketing managers need to be willing to
reconsider past decisions, structures, organisations, and so on, if they
are to have a chance of generating real alternatives.

Further, in analysing alternatives there is no fundamental need
(sometimes there is an operational cost need) to have the same or
similar strategies operating in all product/market areas. It may well
be, for an industrial company selling one product to several end user
markets, that several strategies are needed. In one market, technical
service may be the spearhead, whereas for the same product in another
market, emphasis on a single rugged "take all—do all" part of the
product range may be the most successful. Hand power tools are an
obvious example of this. While a whole range of specialist tools is
supplied to industry, a single, multi-purpose tool may be better for the
home user.

## 2:13  Seeking alternatives by segmentation

The starting point in seeking alternatives is to divide or segment the
markets concerned. The reason for segmenting a market is simply to
choose the ground on which the company has advantages. This is

accomplished by dividing the market into its logical parts and then originating a different approach for each instead of a single attack on the whole market. Further, a company may concentrate on segments of a market in which it receives a proportionately greater gain for a specific effort than it could have received in other segments.

Segmentation policies can be developed for most markets. The simplest segmentations involve user industries concentrating on specific customer applications, geographical areas or size of purchasing company. The advantage of these is that they are easily recognisable.

However, most often the best strategies are based on more meaningful segmentations. There is no doubt that great gains can be made if time and effort is devoted to developing the natural segmentation of a business. The natural segmentation is probably different for each supplier to a market because it involves both the market and the supplier.

Figure 2:7 shows the structure of an industrial control business. It can be seen that segmentation policies could be based on:

1   *User industry.* If for example a company's image was particularly strong in one or other area or they had a sales force already entrenched in one area

2   *Type of system.* Either by problem-solving at one end or by supplying high quality standard equipment or low but acceptable quality equipment for the price conscious. The latter image would almost certainly be incompatible with the former two

3   *Method of operation.* A company could set out to sell answers by customising the equipment package regardless of whose equipment this required, or it could sell its own equipment only

Additional to the above, some markets have discreet price/performance levels. An obvious example is the mobile radio markets. The business of supplying high performance mobile radios to the police, fire, ambulance and other emergency services is quite different from that of supplying mobile radios to taxi companies and similar users. The emergency services need high reliability designs and preventive maintenance. The taxi company is generally satisfied with more basic equipment and a speedy maintenance service in the event of failure.

Analysing customers according to the value of a specific product to them is a further creative segmentation. Indicating instruments for example are often the major visual feature of a complex automation

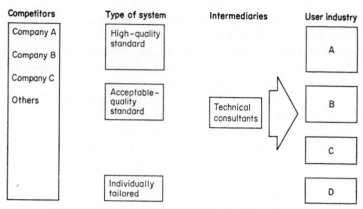

FIGURE 2:7   STRUCTURE OF INDUSTRIAL
CONTROLS BUSINESS
Showing possible Segmentation Policies

panel. Because of this they are a major selling feature of the total installation. The indicating instrument manufacterer who builds good-
looking designs is directly selling a product costing several times the
instrument cost. In such circumstances price pressures are reduced.

Most companies have more than one product and the segmentation
policy needs to take account of the effect of one product on another.
At least the companies in the same division will want to broaden their
range by developing products which are complementary to each other,
such as razor blades and low-cost razors. Few companies offer substitute products unless they are primarily in the business of problem-
solving, when it may be sound marketing policy to offer alternative
solutions. An example would be a company who offered both electronic
and pneumatic solutions to the problem of measuring liquid depths in
process plants. In this way the company can develop an image of problem-solving with impartiality.

The incompatible product can sometimes prove difficult. A precious
metal dealer, for example, introduced a line of chemical sludge pumps.
Their interest lay in the fact that the pumps required an inert lining of
precious metal. However, the image was incompatible and no amount of
promotion would induce purchasers, who all knew the company and
its traditional business, to buy sludge pumps from a precious metal
dealer. A new company, set up as a subsidiary of the precious metal
dealer, but operating independently, sold the pumps successfully.

The various practical alternatives open to the company should now be compared with the projection for the present operations already developed. The actions needed to improve operations are noted.

## 2:14 How value is created

The purpose of creating value is to improve the choice of price strategies available to the company. A review of literature, professional discussions or seminars on business would reveal the enormous effort which has been spent in determining production costs. And yet for most companies this is one of the least important areas in determining the size of profits. The major items are pricing strategy, which determines the size of the total revenue, and purchases, which for the average British manufacturing company take almost 50 per cent of sales revenue.

Pricing is, of course, complex because variations in price affect the number of units sold and therefore the cost breakdown. Nevertheless, the implication holds that pricing and purchasing are the two major areas of business execution. Building toward a price strategy is the major function of marketing. If the markets are already selected, products designed and the marketing mix finalised before price is considered, it is too late to do other than charge competitive prices.

It is essential that price strategies be built around those aspects that are key to the users. In each market there will be a small number of key factors for successful operation. They may be product features that are unique, the type of sales organisation, the physical distribution, manufacturing requirements, or research and development leadership. The key factor for successful operation will be those that give the products their value. Value only exists in the users' hands. Costs can be incurred by the seller, but never value. Costs are set by the producing companies' needs and efficiency. Value is set by the buyers needs and efficiency. A company who finds a cheaper way of manufacturing a product does not reduce that product's value. It may be sensible for him to reduce the price so that the product price is now equal to the value that a wider market places on the product and thus more is sold— but that is quite another question. Competition will, of course, eventually copy a successful product and, often having no other way to compete but on price, they will drive prices down until a level is reached which provides the "normal" cost-plus price levels. Companies need to evaluate how unique their products are and the extent to which this uniqueness is valuable to their customers. This is the only way to achieve above-average profits.

The number of competitors is the crucial factor in determining the extent of price competition already existing in a market. Buyers usually first evaluate suppliers for their compliance with technical specifications. If only two or three companies can meet the technical specification, the market has a good chance of being above average in profitability with the accent on technical development and innovation. If however several suppliers (four or more) can meet the technical specification, competition revolves around commercial factors such as stockholding, delivery, credit, and after sales service. If several companies can also supply these, the buyers can choose on price and the market is of low profit.

Value positions, once created, need to be protected. It is important to determine the positions of strength (proprietary positions) in the market held not only by the company but also by the competition. Some examples of proprietary positions are as follows:

1    Patent protection on products and processes
2    Unique knowhow
3    Unique efficient manufacturing control
4    Unique machinery, parts, supplies, rentals
5    Capture of leading distribution channels
6    Unique customer services, personal selling, executive selling, applications engineering, missionary selling
7    Pioneering a major position
8    Unique marketing techniques
9    Break cost
10   Unique research and development skills
11   Consistently successful new product development

Proprietary positions, therefore, are methods of protecting leadership in the key areas of the market. In a technical market product patents are an obvious example. Xerox, for instance, has held a major lead and built itself into a giant corporation by its tight patent control over a discovery which was the key to a new process. Process knowhow is another form of protected leadership. Companies who pioneer new processes and who can maintain that position attract the type of customer who enables them to conduct further pioneering.

In the marketing arena the pioneering of a major position can bring image advantages which outlast the original lead. Hoover have done this and the name is generic for the product. Ever Ready have captured the leading distribution channels for batteries. Small primary batteries deteriorate on the shelf and at the same time customers expect them to be available in most shops. It is disproportionately economic for the market leader to undertake this and competition has diminished almost completely. Equally it is extremely difficult for others to break in. As a result, manufacturers of electric products design for standard batteries and the process is complete.

Only a few of the methods of obtaining proprietary positions will work in a specific business. The important point is to examine those existing and to consider if any that are not being used would operate.

### 2:15   Seeking methods of creating value

In creating value, the marketing planner needs to look at all the ways in which usefulness to the customer could be improved. The purpose of creativity in a company is to enable the company to charge for its uniqueness. The twin threads of cost-productivity and value-creativity

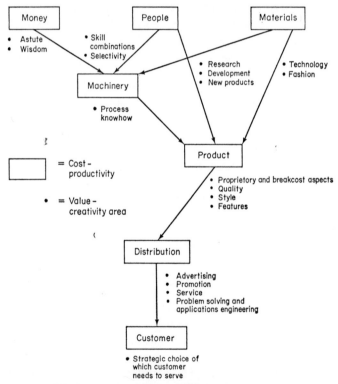

FIGURE 2:8   TWIN THREADS OF COST
PRODUCTIVITY AND VALUE CREATIVITY

are shown in Figure 2:8. It is vital in this to remember that there is no connection between value and cost. In Figure 2:8 there is no connection between the cost of manufacturing, say, production machinery and the innovating skill which makes the machinery both unique and valuable to the customer. Many of the most interesting developments in products, marketing and other business aspects represent creative breakthroughs for the companies concerned. An exciting example, although now ageing, was GKN's entry into the central heating market. They broke most of the rules then existing in the low profit central heating business when they introduced their standardised direct selling Servowarm System together with a fully controlled installation programme. GKN quickly obtained a major share of this fast growing business by reducing costs, saving space to the customer by the use of a standardised system having a master radiator instead of a boiler and cutting out the maze of fuel supplier/builders merchant/installer by direct selling and installation. This is a specific example of profits arising from creative work and not being inherent in the business. Any previous analysis of central heating companies' profits would have shown a very poor picture and if such an analysis had guided GKN they probably would never have entered the business.

All businesses can be of above-average profitability providing the environment enables the company to be in some way unique. Yet how many companies evaluate their positions from a creative standpoint? Costs are analysed and reanalysed. Advertising budgets are increased on existing products in fights with existing competitors. Other companies' successful strategies are applied wholesale to different problems. Product differentials are produced in areas where customers could not possibly be interested. It cannot be emphasised too much that within both the scope of common prudence and customer requirements, companies should set out to be as genuinely different from their competitors as possible. Unorthodox solutions should be explored and an atmosphere of controlled innovation should prevail.

There is also value in differences that do not in reality help the customer. Customers in some markets will be found to be susceptible to appeals featuring quality improvement or unnecessary features and product differentials. A good example of this is in laboratory test equipment. Qualified engineers resent any implication that they are part of a production line and for even simple routine tests will demand oscilloscopes or other measuring instruments which are unnecessarily complex for the job in hand. To be provided with a simplified version demeans their status. In these markets the major shares are almost universally held by the most complex product. The important point is that the customer's need, while perhaps unnecessary, is nevertheless real. Therefore, product differentials appealing to status or any other intangible found in the market will be as genuine as differentials based on real technical need. In the ultimate, there are those who will buy a product just because it is different. Perhaps it is better in profit terms to appeal to this sector than to run third or fourth in the main market segment.

## 2:16  Basic pricing methods

The adoption of a creative approach to marketing demands a change from the usual methods of pricing widely adopted as standard. The three basic methods of pricing are:

1      *Cost plus*. The method is cost oriented and seen generally to be:
   (*a*)  Simple
   (*b*)  Historical
   (*c*)  Effective
   (*d*)  Governmental
   (*e*)  Fair
   (*f*)  Safe
2      *Price theory*. The method concentrates on maximising efficiency. The attempt is to charge the maximum price at which total production can be sold. If demand is high, prices are high. If demand is low, prices are low. The method is:
   (*a*)  Theoretical
   (*b*)  Short range
   (*c*)  In high fixed cost businesses, it is essential to profit
3      *Marketing approach*. The method is oriented toward achieving specific marketing objectives. Its main features are:
   (*a*)  A combination of 1 and 2 above
   (*b*)  Minimises price changes
   (*c*)  Places accent on value
   (*d*)  Major customers determined before price is set
   (*e*)  Uses price to be unique
   (*f*)  Relates price directly to corporate objectives

Cost plus is undoubtedly the most common form, whereby the buyer and seller alike consider that the *fair* price is determined by adding a *reasonable* margin to costs. The cost of this method of pricing to the country must be devastating in terms of lost development. Prices based on costs perpetuate inefficiency and lead to situations whereby more than the true value is paid for some products and no reward is provided for others making products of great value but low cost. The belated discovery of value analysis by buyers can be viewed as an admission of the failure of marketing persons to analyse their users' needs and to price accordingly. A variation of cost plus increasingly being practised is to demand a *fair* return on investment. It is the same principle.

Price theory tries to relate supply and demand. The method is largely theoretical in that data on price elasticity is just not known in most cases and is almost impossible to research. The method is nevertheless a significant advance over cost-plus techniques. It is most applicable to industries which of necessity have a fixed capacity. Jobbing printing for example requires high machine utilisation, and price from one point of view is simply an instrument for maintaining full loading. Hotels, car hire and airlines are further examples of this form of pricing. The disadvantages of the method are that it requires frequent price changes to be workable and is production-oriented at a time when for most companies to be able to produce is not unique.

The marketing approach views pricing as one of the few fundamental determinants of strategy. The ability to give value is considered first. That is when marketing objectives are set in terms of the segments to be served and the user needs on which the company will concentrate. Following this path makes the task of achieving the company's needs in terms of profit and growth easier. In this way, prices are then set not only to obtain a return on that particular sale but also to convey a message to the customer about the company, its quality, its care or its mass production. In practice, this results in prices that appear a cross between cost-plus and price theory methods.


## 2:17   Marketing approach to pricing

The marketing approach allows for the use of several sub-strategies depending on competitive conditions:

1      Penetration pricing
2      Skimming price strategies
3      Diversionary pricing

Penetration price levels are those that will only be profitable at specified and usually high sales levels. It would only be considered as a strategy when the position of market leader is expected to be sufficiently dominant for the company to raise prices later. For example, with perishable products depending on wide distribution, unattractive (to the producers) initial prices will keep out competition while volume is being built. Once achieved, the market leaders' position of strength over the distribution channels is used to hold out competition while price levels (on "new" products or "extra power" variations) are raised. If competition is unlikely to follow quickly, there is little point in this method. A recent example is the Sundstrand Corporation in America who halved their current price of hydraulic motors in order to break open the market for hydrostatic transmissions. No other company has yet dared follow. When and if the market opens up Sundstrand's lead could be dominant.

Skimming price strategies begin with high prices and, as demand builds, the price is reduced. Prices can also be lowered just as competition enters. In this way the leader can often recover a large part of his investment before competition materialises. The competitors, at the new price levels, find difficulty in making a reasonable profit. This method particularly applies to high technology industries where the innovator is not copied immediately and where customers in any case expect prices to fall significantly as new methods of production and so on are discovered.

Diversionary pricing is the strategy of selling one product cheaply so that an associated high profit product is automatically sold. This strategy can be applied to machinery that needs special consumable items or has parts that frequently wear. For example, motor vehicle spares or photocopy machines and the photocopy paper. More recently deep freeze companies have grown up offering special terms on the supply of a deep freeze providing they have the contracts for keeping it provisioned. The strategy will also operate for the same product among different customers. Sparking plugs are often sold at a loss to the motor manufacturers. However, over the vehicle life the owner may buy the same plug retail several times at a totally different price. Diversionary pricing can also be carried out over a product range. Low prices in an area where the company has some special cost advantage can have the effect of worrying competitors whose profits are lower into maintaining price levels across the range.

Not all markets have the freedom of these approaches and yet some are good business in terms of reasonable and stable profits. Usually in these cases a condition of price leadership emerges. One company becomes considered as the leader and if his prices alter all follow. The danger is that a price war may develop. Price wars are won by the market leader or by a large company who can carry the losses either on the other product lines or in some other way. This last is, of course, a variation on penetration pricing.

When selecting the alternative segments and methods of operation which appear to be the most feasible for the company's products, and where selecting the price strategy, it is vital to check the corporate strengths and skills to ensure the company can carry them out. As with the previous section, the actions needed to improve the pricing environment are noted.

## 2:18   The marketing mix

Once the customer target group is identified clearly from the alternative segmentations the various methods of sales communication can be-identified. Broadly, a company purchasing a product passes from realisation of the need, through awareness of the methods of satisfying the need, to conviction as to what specific make of item to buy. The marketing mix needs to be designed for each specific situation. Purchasers of fuel oil clearly do not require to be made aware of their need for fuel oil or the various alternatives to satisfy the need. What is required is a programme aimed at showing which specific make should be purchased. Manufacturers of fluidic devices, however, have a re-education job to undertake. Many possible users have been made aware of the supposed vast potential for fluidics which has become in many ways a fashion that is rapidly going out of date. This has left a legacy of wrong ideas which need first to be eliminated if the correct realisation of the products potential is to be established. Concentration in this case should be on selling the subject primarily and the make secondly.

The first step in the marketing mix is to establish the target person in the buying company. Few purchasing decisions are the result of one man: most require a combination of expertise. The individuals who provide this expertise, whether formally in purchasing or value analysis committees, or informally, are the decision making unit. In almost 90 per cent of companies, three or more departments are involved to a major extent in purchasing. [Hugh Buckner, *How British Industry Buys*, Hutchinson Marketing Library, Roneo Award for best marketing book of 1968, Institute of Marketing.] Members of the decision-making unit are also taking decisions on other aspects which may affect the purchasing decision on the product in question. For the average industrial product it is 1.4 years from the realisation of the need until the purchase is made. [National Industrial Advertisers Association USA.] Clearly during this time many associated decisions are made to a particular purchase which become irreversible in time because of still later actions. Thus an early decision to use, say, electrical rather than hydraulic operation would ultimately exclude a host of hydraulic components. These later manufacturers would have been better promoting hydraulics rather than their company name (Figure 2.9).

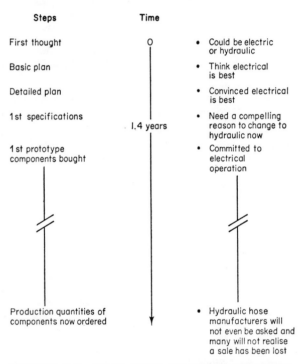

| Steps | Time | |
|---|---|---|
| First thought | 0 | • Could be electric or hydraulic |
| Basic plan | | • Think electrical is best |
| Detailed plan | | • Convinced electrical is best |
| 1st specifications | 1.4 years | • Need a compelling reason to change to hydraulic now |
| 1st prototype components bought | | • Committed to electrical operation |
| Production quantities of components now ordered | | • Hydraulic hose manufacturers will not even be asked and many will not realise a sale has been lost |

FIGURE 2:9 TIME SPAN OF DEVELOPMENTS IN PRODUCING A NEW PACKAGING MACHINE

A selling company needs to study the persons in the decision-making unit—where they fit in, on which factors their decisions are based, how they think and how they like to be approached.

The essential in a well designed marketing programme is to have all aspects of the mix (catalogues and advertisements for example) reinforcing each other inside the decision making unit. It is not important

| | SOME CHARACTERISTICS OF THE STAGE | SOME POSSIBLE STRATEGIES |
|---|---|---|
| Stage 1 | • Unknown, uncertainty, high risk of failure<br><br>• Slow customer acceptance<br>• Wide range of pricing and marketing strategies available | • Plan to be second, maintain close customer contact, pursue acquisition strategy for entry<br>• Create favourable first impression, distribution organised for technical service, introduce a fashion element<br>• Skimming price strategy lengthens life cycle but brings in competition, licensing competitors to produce product, maintains careful quality control and competitive status quo but brings good profits |
| Stage 2 | • Sales run ahead of production, companies tend to product orientation, competitors enter market, originator loses market share<br>• Distribution channels (advisers, consultants, architects) become important<br>• Competition dictates limits of strategies | • Develop brand image<br>• Accent on customer service<br>• Change distribution channels to those able to promote and give wide distribution<br>• Change from "skimming" price strategy towards "competitor exclusion" strategy |
| Stage 3 | • Market saturation is approached. Sales grow at rate of user industries<br>• Fine, almost non-existent product differentials are developed<br>• Price competition becomes intense, new entrants have more modern machinery | • Hold or increase market share by "back selling"— communicating direct with end user. Accent on packaging and advertising to promote more frequent use<br>• Develop other uses amongst existing customers<br>• Develop new markets<br>• Diversify from strengths |
| Stage 4 | • Over capacity develops, production becomes concentrated<br>• Prices and margins fall, suicidal strategies followed with each competitor believing he will be the survivor | • Defensive mergers and acquisitions<br>• Integrate forward—seek added value<br>• Introduce elements of style and fashion<br>• You should not be in this business |

FIGURE 2:10 STAGES IN THE LIFE CYCLE AND
POSSIBLE CHANGES IN MARKET STRATEGY

or even desirable to have each component telling the same complete story. It is only essential that the complete story is clear within the decision making unit. This effect has been likened to conducting an orchestra. While most instruments can play a melody individually a symphony demands that each only plays at set times and in such a way that they complement each other. Unfortunately, many marketing campaigns sound as though all instruments are playing together. Analysis of who makes which decisions based on what factors coupled with how each group prefers to receive data will show how the basic elements of the marketing mix should be organised. In this way design engineers who make decisions on basic systems would, for example, be sold fluidics as a method of control while buyers and operating management would be sold a specific make.

The position of a product in its life cycle obviously has an important bearing on the marketing mix. This is rarely forgotten for a new product but often the market strategy changes needed through a product's life are ignored. Figure 2.10 indicates some possible changes. Figure 2.11 shows the elements of the marketing mix.

### 2:19   Relating corporate objectives to market planning

This chapter has dealt with the company's likely performance in its present products and the alternatives that could optimise sales and profits before coming to corporate objectives. That is the recommended approach. Only when those matters have been fully investigated should the implications of the company's corporate objectives be assessed.

Corporate objectives are now taken as fundamental to good management. Nevertheless, few companies set more than budget targets designed to fulfil specific tactical or operational programmes. At the other end of the scale, all policy makers consciously or unconsciously forge their company into the combined shape of their own needs, values and motivations. In the absence of a clear understanding of the meanings, in terms of business action, of their objectives, marketing managers can only set targets for specific activities and leave the real purpose of the company to develop by chance. A correct appraisal of corporate needs and their translation into meaningful objectives is a vital input to marketing strategy.

The objectives needed for market planning purposes fall into seven areas. Corporate officers who fail to discuss these in detail with the marketing manager are risking the development of final marketing

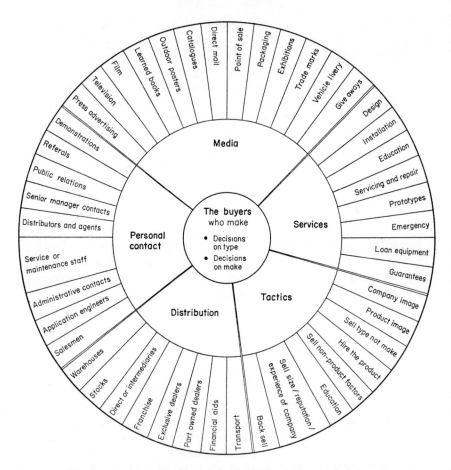

FIGURE 2:11   ELEMENTS OF THE MARKETING MIX

plans which may be far removed from their own ideas of corporate development. The areas are:

1    Targets ahead for sales, profit and capital employed
2    Short term objectives possibly conflicting with longer term objectives but which nevertheless need to be met
3    Stated programmes for each specific business area (how they see it developing)
4    Long-range concept of what the company is doing

5    How balance is to be achieved in objectives where they clash, such as customer service *versus* profits. Practical statements are needed, not panaceas

6    Action guidelines and examples of major policies (staff or company image)

7    Identification of the key result areas (how marketing success is to be judged)

Obviously much data aid and opinion will be needed from marketing personnel in determining the above. But it should be clear that helping set objectives is part of developing corporate strategy, not market planning. If this distinction is not made, planning will descend into the realm of budget forecasting—simply scheduling activities so as to do a bit better than last year. For example, while obviously the likely performance ahead of the existing products is a prime input into any form of realistic target setting, it is not the only one. Corporate needs, in terms of the ambition of the policy makers or the needs of investors, may demand higher targets than can be achieved from the present operations. Equally, the ability of the company to finance the achievement of higher targets depends on the likely cash flow ahead from the present business. All this is further proof of the circular nature of planning and the realistic need to set objectives after the likely sales ahead for the present products have been computed.

## 2:20  Seeking new sources of earnings

The gap between corporate objectives ahead in terms of profit and the likely results ahead for the present products needs to be filled by new sources of earnings. Some companies will plan to fill part of the gap by completely new businesses. These, of course, do not form part of the marketing plan. But part may need to be filled by expansion within the business area of the present products. This will fall into the marketing plan. Further, all products and services follow a life cycle. An active policy of developing new sources of earnings within the present market areas is, if nothing else, essential to ensure survival.

There is no doubt that the need for new business and the specific directions in which it should be sought arises from the company's own position and not primarily from the availability of "good" opportunities in the environment. Despite this, many companies' new earnings programmes (formal or informal) are based on an external search for likely opportunities which are then considered as to their compatibility with the existing operation. This type of approach leads to:

1    Lack of corporate commitment and therefore action
2    Hasty and ill-founded decisions
3    Agreement to "diversification" so long as it is small

There are, however, several well tried methods of generating new sources of earning from a company's own products and markets by using the company's strengths and unique abilities. These have several powerful advantages over the "let's keep our eyes open for something good" variety:

1    They utilise a company's key existing abilities and there-
      fore base new developments soundly
2    Being developed from the company using its unique
      aspects, they avoid the bandwagon effect where many
      companies all rush into the same apparently good external
      opportunity. By the same reasoning they avoid the profit
      squeeze which results from bandwagon competition
3    These methods locate profit opportunities close to the
      company's present marketing operations in terms of
      products (or services), markets or technologies

The methods depend on identifying the opportunities available for the company's existing strengths. Put another way, the company seeks new opportunities which are in some way linked to the present operations. Obvious moves are selling the existing products to new markets or further products to existing customers. However, for companies strong in areas such as applications engineering, there may be opportunities not with present customers or present products but with others which, because they have a high applications engineering content, may legitimately be regarded as closely related to the present marketing operation.

It is readily accepted that market studies can be undertaken to show in great detail the various market opportunities for a product. It is not so readily understood that markets can equally easily be studied for a strength. For example a speciality paper company having skills in long fibre technology and related adhesives would probably have advantages over competitors in all areas where fibres are fixed using adhesives. In this way the strengths are turned into "product market" scope definitions. Thus the need for adhesives would suggest "fabricated non-woven fibre products." Such a product/market scope would cover not only increasing quantities of medical products such as tissues, towels, swabs and so on, but also consumer items such as home tissues and extend to such areas as flocculated carpets. Each resulting product/market area is evaluated to show:

1   Marketing characteristics
2   Competition
3   Principal market segments
4   Product characteristics
5   Feasibility of entry
6   New skills needed
7   Market size
8   Market growth
9   Opportunity for profit
10  Compatibility
11  Risk

The resulting product/markets are then placed in order of attractiveness.

Having chosen the priority areas there are four basic methods of market entry. In some cases, combinations of methods can be used:

1   Developing new products
2   Acquiring licences
3   Acquiring specialist skills
4   Purchase of companies

Internal development of new products is probably the highest risk method of market entry. Development times are long and the rate of new product failure high. However, the return on investment when successful is the highest of the four methods. New product development is discussed in chapter 3.

Acquiring licences is feasible when another country is further ahead in technical and marketing development. The problem is that licence fees often continue to reduce what were above average profits to merely average (see chapter 3).

Acquiring specialists is a key method of entry in those markets where skills and services are more important in terms of product differential than physical properties of the products. Capital investment is low—but specialists can be temperamental and leave and the original search may have been lengthy. See chapters 4 and 5 on manpower planning.

Marketing planners may wish to recommend the purchase of companies in order to achieve market entry. Good companies are rare however and often the subject of many offers already. Nevertheless, the speed and low risk of acquisition can, when reasonable growth rates are achieved, be coupled with a reasonable return on investment (see chapter 6).

## 2:21 The market plan

The steps taken to this point have been analysis rather than the market plan itself and many factors needing to be altered have been simply noted. This is important. At all stages, specific points and alternatives are reconsidered, later ideas being allowed to impact on those which have gone before, and so on. The marketing planners must first feel that all aspects have been examined and the alternatives which optimise both existing products and developments determined before they draw together the actions which will be needed to carry these intentions into effect. These actions are the marketing plan. Naturally, the actions will be different for differing products, markets and divisions. There is no essential virtue in building up identical volumes for each product/ market in each division covering say, sales plans, promotion plans, advertising plans, and so on. The action in each area will be different —the plans should differ. Notes of discussions, meetings or other reasoning sessions should however be kept in a "back-up file" so that the chain of reasoning can be reconstructed. At this stage therefore all the process should be reviewed and the actions needed to effect changes listed under the headings:

1  Action needed
2  Benefit
3  Cost to solve
4  Decision deadline
5  Priority

The expected benefits and costs should be estimated and time schedules determined. This will show the priorities among the actions. Probably it will also show that a number of actions which seemed right in themselves do not warrant management time in view of higher priorities. These low priority actions should be rejected. Next, each action needs to be allocated to an individual—the action assignee. The specific actions should be entered on a form similar to that shown in Figure 2:12.

| Action assignee: | | | | | | |
|---|---|---|---|---|---|---|
| Control assignee: | | | | | | |

| Resource schedule | 1971 | 1972 | 1973 | 1974 | 1975 |
|---|---|---|---|---|---|
| | J F M A M J J A S O N D | J F M A M J J A S O N D | | | |
| Description: | | | | | |

Results schedule

Description of control system

FIGURE 2:12  ASSIGNMENT FORM
Showing the actions required to implement the market plan
and the individuals to whom each action has been assigned

Planning form sets help considerably in the physical development of a marketing plan. They can be designed to lead management through all the steps described in this chapter.

The individual who is to control the assignment (the control assignee) is also inserted on the form and the method of control specified. The costs are placed at the points where they are planned to occur, as are the results expected. Once all actions are assigned, two important rescheduling tasks can be undertaken. These are designed to ensure:

1   That no individual has an impossibly high work load

2        That there is no undue "bunching" in either costs or
         benefits which would cause cash flow problems.

Following such rescheduling, the forms shown in Figure 2:12 are,
together with a brief statement of the objectives and strategy in each
area, the marketing plan.

# THREE

# New Product Planning

*by T S McLeod*

There are a few industries in which the same products may be sold year after year without any serious changes. Distilling and paper making are examples. But in the great majority a constant stream of new products is essential. In some cases the urgency is obvious: an aeroplane manufacturer must be working on a new model before the current one has reached its first customer; at the other extreme, a milliner is little better off. In other cases, a product may last for several years and the timing of a successor is a matter for careful thought. The common factor is that sooner or later new products must replace existing ones and that unless they are developed in time the business will die.

The planning problems with existing products or even products of a similar nature are comparatively simple. The markets are known: the prices that may be expected can be predicted with some confidence. More serious difficulties come when a company decides to embark on what amounts to a new line of business. The approaches that should be adopted in planning follow very similar lines in both cases but there is a crucial difference. A decision to enter a new area is made only if the estimated costs of development and manufacture show a high probability of profitable sales. A decision not to continue in an existing area is made only if it can be established beyond a reasonable doubt that it will not be possible to remain there profitably.

Planning should aim at reducing to a minimum the hazards of entering a new area of activity. This can be done by choosing products which exploit new techniques in known markets, or known techniques in new ones. Every new venture depends on a belief that predictions will be as good as those of competitors. This is unlikely to be true unless at least part of the ground is familiar.

## 3:1 Generating new product ideas

Before discussing how new product proposals should be assessed and implemented, it is useful to consider how they originate. In the broadest sense they all arise in the same way. Thinking about the changes taking place in their business, people talk to one another and ideas emerge. In many small companies this is sufficient: in large companies it is necessary to take the formal steps described in later paragraphs to ensure that the right stimulation is applied and that no possible idea is lost. The stimulus for new product ideas can arise from any source. Here it will be sufficient to indicate these areas in which new product discussions take place and the type of proposal that emerges.

Technical and scientific advances provide a major source of new products. The people who are engaged in research and development are in touch with these advances. They must keep up to date by reading, and by attending conferences over the widest possible field, and they must have frequent discussions with marketing and planning experts. Between them they will see ways in which new techniques can lead to new products.

An equally prolific source lies in the market itself. People develop new requirements, they think of new ways of spending their money, fashions come and go. Salesmen are often the first to see new possibilities but their ideas need to be examined by economists and accountants. For example, tape recorders have been available for a very long time and a lot of people would get pleasure from one, but it is only in communities which combine a particular level of spending power and social pressure that they can be sold in quantity.

Developments in manufacturing techniques are no less important. There are a lot of products like ball point pens which sell in very small quantities when priced at several pounds and in very large quantities when they are available for a few pence. Here again neither the marketing man nor the production engineer is likely to come up with a good new idea on his own. It is in discussion between them that it will emerge and that the ten bad ideas which surround every good one can be painlessly killed.

Without this constant, uninhibited discussion between everyone in a business, the company will soon run short of new ideas. No one individual or department can be expected to supply them alone. Nor will new product ideas appear at all unless everyone who has something to contribute knows sufficient of the general plans and policies of the company to understand the sort of new products that it needs. The responsibility that can be put upon an individual or department is to ensure that all the proposals that are generated are channelled to a point at which they are properly analysed and that a decision is made on each.

### 3:2   The task of research and development

The success of a new product plan depends on the correct use of technical staff and this in turn depends on an understanding of the several functions which they should fulfil. This work contains four quite different sorts of activity commonly described as basic research, applied research, development and design. (There is some confusion in nomenclature: applied research is sometimes described as advanced development and design is sometimes called engineering or product development. The names are not important so long as the four stages are recognised.)

*Basic research.* As carried out in universities, institutions and in private industry, basic research is an attempt to extend the frontiers of human knowledge. Its outstanding characteristic is that it is an open activity. Workers publish their results, describe them at conferences, and exchange laboratory visits, so that new discoveries are soon available to everyone who is interested. This compensates for the fact that progress in any one place is slow, laborious and unpredictable. The amount that any one man discovers is very small and his value to his company is that his work in the field gives him access to the work of hundreds of others. His job is to bring to the notice of his company anything, no matter where or by whom it is discovered, that may affect the future of the business.

It may seem anomalous to employ a man on projects which offer little hope of any direct return to his company in the hope that he will enable it to exploit the work of research workers in other places. An apparent alternative would be to employ people who did no work of their own, simply trying by reading journals and attending conferences to get the information that is required. In practice this would not work. The papers presented at conferences are usually neither complete nor exhaustive and are in any case many months out of date by the time they are discussed. Far better information comes from direct contacts with men who are working in the same technical area. They are always eager to talk to anyone who has results of his own to describe and will often follow the discussions with invitations to their laboratories. The man who has nothing of his own to contribute will not be offered anything in exchange. The entrance fee to the international commonwealth of scientific research is to make a contribution to it.

The proper projects for the basic research laboratories of a company to undertake are any that will give them access to the areas of scientific advance that are most likely to affect the future of the business. The main duty of the staff is to be thoroughly familiar with all of their company's activities and to bring to its notice immediately any scientific advance, no matter where or by whom it is made, that may affect them. The way in which this activity may be harnessed to new product development is discussed in paragraph 3.7.

*Applied research.* The function of applied research is entirely different. It starts with a phenomenon or technique which may possibly be of some use to a company. It ends when it has quantified, extended and defined the new phenomenon or technique to the point at which a preliminary specification for a product in which it is to be incorporated may be prepared.

Effective use of research and development effort depends on a clear distinction between basic and applied research projects. The former are chosen simply to have a team in the right technical area and with sufficient personal knowledge to gain access to the international scene. The latter are chosen with a firm intention that if they achieve their objective it will lead to the development of a definite product at a foreseeable time. They are therefore characterised by clear statements of what the team is aiming to do and a date by which they are required to do it. One or both of these things may be amended as the work goes forward, but at a given moment they must both be quite definite.

*Development.* The process is carried further forward by development, which is usually the most important and critical stage. It gathers together the new knowledge that research has produced and combines it with previously existing techniques to establish the feasibility of a complete design. It is often treacherously easy to show that something will work on its own. To make it work as part of a complete system, under all the conditions that it will encounter and in such a way that it will meet economic requirements as well as technical ones, can be a great deal harder.

In some cases it is sufficient to produce laboratory models of certain parts of a new product. In others a complete feasibility model is required. The criterion of completion for a development project is that all the uncertainties should have been removed and that it should put into the hands of the designer all the information that he needs. From that stage onward, he should not need to leave the drawing board.

*Design.* Far from being the process of specifying and describing a new product, design is the preparation of a plan for making it. It introduces the aesthetic and ergonomic factors which play little part in development and it depends for its success on an intimate knowledge of manufacturing methods. It provides the crucial link between research and development and production.

### 3:3   Obtaining new products under licence

Increasing communications has made it very much easier than it used to be to license products from other companies, particularly overseas companies, and this has become common in the more sophisticated sectors of industry. In planning it must always be considered as a possible alternative to in-house development. There are several reasons why this may be done and each one of them has its own combination of advantages and hazards.

*Saving of time.* It often seems possible to save time by buying working drawings from another firm and to use them immediately in production rather than to go through the long, hard development process. The initial down payment on the licence can be much less than the cost of development, and royalties on sales have to be paid only if the product is successful.

The dangers are that protracted negotiations bite into the time saved, initial production difficulties are slow to clear when the designers are not easily accessible, costs tend to be higher than the licensors predicted and the additional burden of royalties may make the product unprofitable.

*Technical leaders.* A better ground for licensing a product is that it is technically in advance of anything available locally. This is a common reason for the production under licence of American designs in Europe and European designs in the other continents. It can be extremely profitable to both parties. The licensee gets a product that he can sell at a premium price in a market in which there is no competition, while the licensor gets an immediate down payment followed by a steady income without the trouble, expense and uncertainty of setting up selling or manufacturing facilities in another country.

The main hazard is that advanced technical products are difficult to make and the unavailability of the original designers is an even more severe drawback than it is for simpler products. The technical lead may prove short-lived and another local manufacturer who has done his own development may well offer a cheaper product when he appears on the market. Even the market can be treacherous. Customers can be remarkably disinclined to pay extra for technical excellence and may continue to buy inferior but cheaper products.

These difficulties notwithstanding, a genuine technical lead over anything on the local market is the most powerful argument for planning a licensing agreement.

*Political choices.* There are very few countries which allow completely free competition between home manufactured and imported goods. This is sometimes because of difficulty in balancing their overseas payments and sometimes for military or prestige reasons.

Balances of payments fluctuate rapidly and plans based upon favourable conditions produced by the exclusion or encouragement of particular imports or exports must be treated with caution. Military considerations provide a more secure foundation. Every country is anxious to supply its armed forces from factories under its own control and in particular to avoid imports which must make long sea voyages. National prestige is almost equally important. Governments are among the largest customers of the aircraft, electronic and communication industries and they have a marked tendency to prefer goods manufactured in their own countries.

These situations give excellent opportunities for profitable licensing. When there is no native capability for the manufacture of a sophisticated product and where imports are unacceptable to the main customer, there is an ideal situation for manufacture under licence from overseas.

*Business development.* Any of these reasons may justify the initial step of taking a licence. They will seldom give a company more than a temporary lead over competitors. If the product is successful, other people will take licences from other originators and they will usually be able to negotiate better terms than the first company to enter the field. The best way to withstand this competition is to use the new product as a base upon which to build a development and design competence. This may either make possible a break-away from the original licensor or may lead to a two way exchange of help and information. Either way, long term success can be built only on adequate technical backing at the point of manufacture. Licensing can be a good way to get into a new line of business, but by itself it will not sustain it for long.

The important thing in each case is that the decision to license a product should be made on a clear understanding of the advantages and hazards that it offers, using the same criteria as are applied to products developed in-house. There are two additional reasons for which it may be chosen:

1    It will get into production faster than an internally developed one could, and thus fill a gap in production commitments
2    It will have a market advantage due to political decisions

These must be considered as support for one or another of the considerations discussed in section 3.13, not as a substitute for them. Neither can, by itself, justify the manufacture of a product which is not viable in its own right.

## 3:4  Fundamental limitations in adopting new product ideas

No product planning process is open-ended. Each has certain boundaries within which it must operate and the first step in new product planning is to determine what these limitations are.

In capital intensive industries the limitation is a simple one. At a particular time there is a certain manufacturing capacity available. If it is fully loaded the business is likely to be profitable. If it is not fully loaded, overhead and depreciation costs will be very little reduced and there is a high probability that these will swamp any savings that can be made elsewhere. Consequently a first criterion in new product planning is to select those products whose development can be timed to keep manufacturing capacity fully loaded. A decision to increase capacity will take a long time to implement, besides calling for new capital, negative cash flow, building permits and other things. If it is made it will become necessary to provide additional products at the right time.

In either event the new product plans must be based on the loading requirements of the factory. Within reasonable limits the individual profitability of a product is of secondary importance.

There are circumstances in which manufacturing capacity can be expanded quickly. In these cases there are other limitations. It may be that a trained sales force can handle only a certain volume of business and that to expand it would be impracticable or might lead to retaliatory action by competitors. In this case the object of planning will be to provide just enough activity to keep the sales force loaded.

In another field the size of the market is determined by political. considerations. A government will buy a certain number of nuclear submarines each year and there may be nothing to be gained by offering an alternative design.

Yet another limitation lies in the development team available. They have certain skills and facilities. A decision to recruit more men or to build larger laboratories will not begin to affect the rate of progress on development projects for many months. Too rapid recruitment may even reduce output as the newcomers take up the time of established staff.

Finally, there are financial restrictions. Development spending may be limited. Products which produce a favourable cash flow within a short period may be given priority over those that will be more profitable in the long term.

It is only when these overriding priorities have been settled that new product planning can begin.

## 3:5   The basics of new product selection

Subject to the overriding limitations discussed in the last paragraph, the first criterion by which a proposed new product should be judged is the extent to which it exploits the assets which may be expected to give its parent company an advantage over competitors.

Money, unskilled labour and standard types of plant are available to many people and may be termed *simple assets*. Special skills, advanced machinery and experienced development teams are available to very few and may be termed *differentiated assets*. The new products which are likely to be successful are the ones which make the greatest demand on these differentiated assets and the least demand on the simple ones.

Even in terms of apparently simple assets such as money, unspecialised plant and unskilled labour, companies may have differentiating advantages. A new product may initially produce a large negative cash flow or require efficient use of a great deal of plant and labour.

For one company, these factors may present no serious problem and the product is therefore a good one. For a company which lacks the necessary financial reserves or the plant, supervisory staff and labour, however, it would be inadvisable to attempt to develop this particular product.

Whatever the current assets of a company, the prime purpose of new product planning must be to exploit them to the maximum and to make the minimum demand for additional ones. Failure to plan new products in such a way that differentiated assets are fully committed is equivalent to throwing away the best cards in a hand.

### 3:6   Reasons for customer appeal in new products

The new product planning process would be very much easier if customers made the decision to buy or not to buy on simple, rational grounds. Unfortunately, their motives are usually mixed and sometimes irrational. In formulating new product policy it is useful to distinguish a number of possible reasons for which a customer will choose a particular product, but it should not be forgotten that in practice the decision will seldom depend upon one of them alone. Five of the most important are:

1   The product performs some function better than anything else available
2   The demand for the product is so great that the total productive capacity available is taken up
3   The product can be made better or more cheaply than competitive products
4   The sales force has established a situation with its customers which will ensure that they buy the new product
5   Confidence in the supplier, habit or "brand loyalty" will ensure that certain customers accept the new product

In the sections that follow each of these factors is examined in turn.

### 3:7   Value of technical leadership

It has been said that if you make a better mousetrap the world will beat a way to your door. It is unlikely that anybody who believes this will have accumulated enough money to buy a book like this. Technically advanced products have to be sold with just as much vigour as those with any other merit. The point is that once the attention of a potential customer has been drawn or even forced to them, it is their technical superiority that will lead him to buy.

Examples abound. There are aircraft and razor blades, nuclear power plants and golf balls, computers and plastic macs which are better than their competitors. The first key point is that each one is better only for a particular purpose and for a particular customer. An aircraft is optimised for a certain pay load and type of journey: a razor blade for a certain beard and set of shaving conditions. There are no absolute bests. Each technical merit must be assessed in terms of the size of market to which it will appeal.

The second key point is that a technical lead of any real value will not last. Scientific knowledge is too widely spread and the protection offered by patent laws is too weak for the appearance of competitive products to be more than a matter of time.

These considerations define the three questions which must be asked when a new product is proposed on the grounds of its technical superiority:

1    How many customers will be attracted by the technical
     advantages of the new product?
2    How much will they be willing to pay for these advant-
     ages?
3    Does this return justify the development cost?

Only if the answers to these questions are favourable does technical superiority become a really valuable asset.


## 3:8   Effect of market conditions

It is sometimes said that all product decisions must depend on market considerations. This is a truism which is dangerous in its omissions. All decisions must take account of technical, manufacturing and many other factors, and it is important to identify the limited number for which the market considerations are dominant. These are the ones which deal with products which will sell profitably although their technical qualities or manufacturing methods are no better than those of competitors. Conversely there are some which cannot be sold profitably in spite of superior technical qualities and manufacturing methods. There are examples of both. One extreme is presented by war-time conditions in which the demand for consumer goods is great and the manufacturing capacity available to meet it is small. Anyone who can muster the plant and materials to make anything can sell it. The other extreme is represented by conditions of acute depression such as the early nineteen thirties in which there was so little purchasing power in the community that the best products were often unsaleable. Consider four examples typical of prosperous peacetime:

**1** In the early nineteen fifties in England, television had been available for nearly fifteen years, apart from the war-time break. It had made only limited progress, because sets were too expensive for large sectors of the community and programmes insufficiently attractive for many of the others. Reduction in the cost of sets, increasing wage levels, better hire purchase facilities and an improvement in programme quality coincided to produce an explosion in demand. For seven or eight years it was possible to sell television sets faster than they could be produced and the industry was highly profitable. Then, quite suddenly, the point was reached at which virtually everyone who wanted a set had one, and only the replacement market remained. The available productive capacity was too great and profits collapsed as companies fought for the disappearing business, trying desparately to keep their production lines efficiently loaded.

**2** The demand for telephone equipment has followed the same initial pattern but is so far showing no sign of saturation. This is mainly because although it is reasonably simple for anyone with experience of radio manufacture to set up a line to make television sets, telephone equipment poses harder problems. The capital equipment and engineering competence required are of a higher order, and several years are likely to elapse between the entry of a newcomer to the business and his first deliveries. Consequently the supply of equipment has been limited by the ability of the traditional suppliers to build new factories and to train new labour. Even when they have been able to do this there has been a gap of years between a decision to go ahead and the appearance of a higher rate of output. The intervening period has shown a classical picture of a market willing to take everything that could be produced.

**3** A contrasting situation has been that of the electrical power industry. An overoptimistic view of the rate at which the demand for electricity would increase has resulted in the existence in several countries of more manufacturing capacity for generating plant than the responsible authorities have been willing to order. In this situation it is almost impossible for any supplier to operate profitably.

**4**  A less sophisticated example is that of tinned cat food. Thirty years ago, cats fed on scraps and caught mice when they were hungry. In post-war years efficient refrigeration and cheap canning processes made it possible to produce tins of low quality protein very cheaply. At the same time an increasing number of cat owners had money to spare and had been conditioned to respond to pseudo-scientific advertising that told them that they were doing less than their duty to a pet if they did not feed it from a tin. The result has been to produce a generation of cats who associate food with tin openers, and who catch vermin only to present the bodies as trophies to their owners.

The degree of marketing skill that created this industry should not be underestimated. The technology had to be there: the customers had to have money in their pockets: the advertising campaign had to reach people who would be convinced by it: the cats had to be adaptable. No market survey, no theoretical analysis could have produced the information. It was a straight case of imaginative thinking and efficient application.


These examples illustrate the nature of market-inspired product decisions. The key factors are a prediction of market demand and an estimate of the productive capacity that will be available to fill it. The longer the time gap between the decision and the product the greater is the hazard and the more tempting the prize.

It must be emphasised that there are no easy or automatic procedures for getting the right answers. Market surveys tell the enquirer what a potential customer wants at the moment and what he thinks he will want in the future. Experience is that his answers often prove a poor guide. To be successful, a marketing man must know his customer's needs so well that he will himself be able to predict correctly which of the new technical developments that will become available will result in a product which the customer will choose when he sees it. He must foresee the economic, social and political events that will change the market situation. He must be aware of the present capabilities of other manufacturers and must also estimate their future reactions in order to predict the ratio of productive capacity to demand at the times that matter.

The question to be answered may be summarised as follows:


1      What products will be wanted in increasing quantity in the future?

2     What will be the ratio of available manufacturing capacity
      to demand?
3     How long will a position of advantage last?
4     What will be the cost of securing it, and what will be the
      reward?

### 3:9   Making use of manufacturing advantages

It is perfectly reasonable to plan a new product on the grounds that it
will succeed because it will be made more efficiently than competing
products, but the grounds for this belief must be explicit. A pious hope
that things will turn out alright is not enough. There are many possible
reasons for optimism and each must be examined carefully to ensure that
the advantages being gained in one way are not being lost in another.

Special manufacturing skills once played a major part in industrial
success. Craftsmen who could produce non-porous castings or mould
clear glass gave their employers a crucial advantage. In the same way
access to particular types of china clay or other minerals has been the
foundation of whole industries. With the spread of technical knowledge
and the discovery of new sources of materials such instances have become rare. What does remain is a scarcity of particular skills. In theory
anyone can learn to be a toolmaker and they can be recruited anywhere.
In practice they are hard to find and a company who has them has an
asset that can be used to produce a position of advantage.

There is a similar situation with unskilled labour. In some places it is
plentiful and cheap, in others it is neither. There are American firms
which have set up factories in Hong Kong to assemble transistors and
English companies who manufacture electronic components in Portugal,
the saving in labour costs covering the other expenses. Factories like
this are significant assets in the planning of products with a high labour
content. They are of little use for mechanised production. The availability of the labour is not the whole story. The supervisory staff who
can maintain volume and quality of output and the production engineers
who can find ways of making complicated products by a series of simple
operations are an essential ingredient of success and one that cannot be
assembled in a short time.

The situation with plant is more obvious. If there are economies
to be obtained by the use of expensive or unusual machines anyone who
starts out with them has a clear lead. He can be overhauled only by a
competitor who is able to commit the capital cost of making good his

deficiency and even if the money is available the time lag may be significant. This is a point at which good information from sales and marketing is essential. The operating cost of making most things can be reduced by increased investment in tools and machinery. The economic limit depends on the numbers that will be sold and the time at which they will be sold. If the number is large the company which can afford to make the optimum initial investment will gain a crucial manufacturing advantage.

Most things can be improved by working on them and more mechanisation is not the only way. A team skilled in the technique of value engineering and cost reduction can show results on the great majority of products. Here too the investment must be weighed against the return with another limitation. Just as those who have no money to spare cannot buy new tools and machinery, those who have not recruited and trained value engineering teams cannot set them to work on their products.

It should be emphasised that manufacturing costs must be considered as a whole and in direct comparison with competitors. The consideration of a proposed new product must show what it gains and loses in each of the following items:

1    Availability of special skills
2    Cost and supply of labour
3    Production engineering and supervision
4    Optimum mechanisation and tooling
5    Value engineering and cost reduction

### 3:10    Assessing the salesman's advice

It is a common boast among salesmen that although they have never had the right product at the right time, they have always sold it. This illustrates the essential difference between marketing and selling. The object of the first is to find the products that will sell themselves; that of the second is to persuade customers to take what is available.

There are many new products which have no significant advantages over those offered by competitors and their success depends almost entirely on the efforts of the sales force. It is important that the design should take full account of the factors which are of most assistance to them.

The relationship of a salesman to his customer is complex. The type of man whose persuasiveness enables him to get rid of an inferior product at a high price and then to move on, is of little use in the long term planning of a business. This must depend on a sales force tha has learned to live with its customers and that has earned their confidence and respect. This can only come from a record of service which is made up partly by the way in which it has reacted to the problems and difficulties that a commercial situation inevitably produces and partly by the quality of the goods that it has supplied in the past. The good salesman establishes a position in which his customers know him well and come to him immediately with any problem that arises. Once they have learned to do this they hesitate to go to anyone else, even someone whose goods appear to have advantages.

The salesman has to face the problem of divided loyalties. His duty to his employers is to sell the goods that they make and not to let a customer call for modifications or "specials". His standing with his customers depends on his ability to persuade his company to give them the service that they want and not to palm them off with something designed for someone else.

This is the clue to the part that salesmen should play in new product planning. They know better than anyone else the things that will make a new product acceptable to the maximum number of customers with a minimum number of variations and options. They can do this better than market analysts and much better than engineers and they should be listened to with respect whenever a new product is being discussed. But it should not be forgotten that their involvement is essentially in the present. Their advice on short term products is vital, but as the time scale stretches it becomes less important. On really long term questions it is quite likely to be bad.

This underlines once more the difference between selling and marketing. There is no question of one being in any way superior to the other. Their functions are different. The salesman should involve himself deeply in his customers' immediate needs and problems. The marketing man should gaze into the future, identifying a customer's future requirements before he becomes aware of them himself. It would be an excellent thing if the same man could do both but it is one of the harsh facts of experience that very few people can. Good planning means using each man's advice where it is most likely to be sound, following the salesman for short term and the marketing man for long term products.

The questions to be asked about a new product proposed by the sales staff may be summarised as follows:

1    Which customers will prefer the new product to an existing company one?

2    Which customers are likely to switch from a competitor and what will the new sales be worth?

3    What reduction in requests for modifications and "specials" will the new product produce? What is the estimated value of this reduction?

4    Will there be any improvement in customer relations as a result of the new product? Is this quantifiable?

5    What will the effect on sales turn-over for each salesman be?

### 3:11   Extent of habit or traditional purchasing

It has been said before that planning would be easier and more effective if people always acted from rational motives. The idea that a customer carries out a full and intelligent analysis of the available products and then chooses the one best suited to his needs and his pocket appears more often in textbooks than in real life. Most people stick to a particular supplier so long as he gives them satisfaction and change only when the reasons for doing so have become overwhelming. There are many reasons for this, even if not all of them are good ones.

The simplest is that familiar problems are easier to handle. The quality of an established supplier's goods, his after-sales service, the reliability of his delivery promises and his reaction to complaints are all known. A new supplier may produce disappointments under any of these headings. A cautious buyer may consider that this uncertainty is too high a price to pay for the apparent advantages offered. Equally important is the phenomenon of acquired taste. A man who is supplied regularly with a particular food, drink or type of tobacco usually develops a preference for it and feels deprived if he does not get it at the accustomed time. It is only necessary to send the trolley round an hour later than usual or to supply the sugar takers with unsugared tea and vice versa to cause a near riot in most offices. Organisations resemble individuals in many ways. Once they have become habituated to a particular product there will be resistance at every level to any change and a prudent management will not provoke it without very good reason.

Intelligent planning exploits these factors to the full. It recognises in its traditional customers a differentiated asset and it gives them preference over new customers in its product planning.

There are dangers as well as advantages in putting reliance on these factors. To keep established markets it is only necessary to be as good as the competition: to break into new markets it is necessary to be significantly better. The danger is that a company which is content to be no better than the next is likely to drift into a position in which it is a good deal worse. There will be a time lag between this deterioration and the loss of its tradition bound customer and by the time that the downward trend becomes unmistakable it will have gone so far that recovery will be long and expensive.

The questions to be asked when a new product is proposed on the grounds that it will maintain traditional markets are:

1   Why will traditional customers want this new product?
2   Does it replace an existing product or does it extend the range?
3   Is it in any way inferior to competitive products?
4   Will it gain any new customers?

### 3:12   Assessing validity of new product proposals

The basis of intelligent action is good information. This consists of facts about the past, which can usually be established with precision, and predictions about the future, each of which should contain an estimate of its accuracy. The information that is required before planning can begin should cover:

1   The development and start up costs of each existing product
2   The past sales of existing products and the predicted future pattern
3   The estimated development and start up costs of each new product
4   The predicted sales of each new product

These patterns are illustrated in Figure 3:1.

It may be protested that planning is concerned with the future and not the past, but this is far from being the case. Every established product was a new product once, and there is no better teacher than history. The first step in assessing the validity of new product proposals is to compare the facts of the past and the present with the predictions which led the company to develop the products that it did. If this is

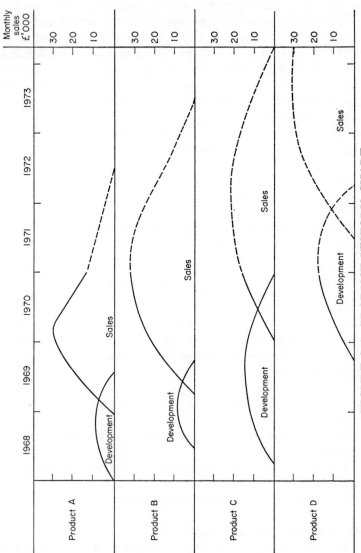

FIGURE 3:1 PRODUCT HISTORY CHART
Showing information required before planning can begin

done carefully and thoughtfully it will usually become clear that some engineers and salesmen are over optimistic and some are over cautious. Some are reasonably accurate in their predictions of costs and sales, others make wild guesses. Each man's predictions of the future must be judged against his past performance, due account being taken of any good reasons that he can give for past mistakes.

Most engineers and salesmen consider themselves to be good forecasters. Unfortunately, this is by no means always true and good planning depends on a recognition of both the strengths and weaknesses of each man in the team. The estimates of a designer or salesman should always be listened to with care and clarified by questioning but the figures that go into the ultimate plan may often have to be qualified by a better judge.

*Producing the new product planning chart.* When individual product proposals have been quantified as accurately as possible it becomes necessary to produce an overall planning chart. This can take many forms but it must carry the information shown in Figure 3:1. To be an effective guide it should go back and forward in time by at least the total life of an average product. The information on the left of the "now" line is fact: that on the right is conjecture. The first provides the background against which the credibility of the second can be assessed. It tells a manager:

1   Which products required excessive development expenditure
2   Which products had too short a life
3   What the rate of rise or fall in sales of present products is likely to be

The information on right hand side gives forecasts of future developments and shows:

1   Future development costs
2   The extent to which new products will fill the gaps left by the obsolescence of old ones
3   The times at which changes in production or sales techniques will be required

These predictions must be tested and the way to test them is to ask questions.

The first question to ask is why a product was bought by a customer. The reasons must be quantified as accurately as possible. The same questions must then be asked about each new product that has been proposed and the answer set against the sales forecasts. It is possible to do this and still to get the wrong answers, but if it is not done the possibility becomes a near certainty.

A critical appreciation of development forecasts is just as difficult. It is essential to check an engineer's present prediction against the outcome of his past ones but this is only a partial guide. He may have learnt some lessons or an older estimate may have been a lucky guess. Either way, his proposals should be set out on a control chart (see page 95) and each item on it scrutinised in detail. When this is done it is usually found that much of the development is of a routine nature and capable of accurate prediction and that the areas of genuine uncertainty are small enough for the total estimate to be within acceptable limits of accuracy.

### 3:13　New product selection

It has been necessary to consider the product planning chart in its final form before examining the reasons for selecting some possible new products and rejecting others. This has been done because the chart illustrates many of the factors which determine the final selection. From it can be calculated:

1　　The future load on research and development facilities
2　　The future load on production capacity
3　　The degree to which each of the company's available assets will be utilised
4　　The demand for additional facilities

It is worth recalling the absolute limits on the selection of projects mentioned in paragraph 3:4. The load on research and development facilities must not be greater than can be carried by those that are available or can be made available. The same applies to production facilities. New plant can be obtained only if the money is there to buy it and if suppliers can deliver it in time.

Statements of this sort may seem to be perfectly obvious. The essential thing is that until the demands on resources which each existing and each proposed product will make have been plotted out and the quantities totalled, it is not possible to see whether plans are capable of fulfilment.

The usual result of such calculations is to show that there are various ways of using the company's development resources that satisfy the criteria described above, particularly as there is likely to be some flexibility in the amount of production capacity that can be made available at a time some distance in the future. The factors on which a choice should be made have been indicated in earlier sections and they may now be put in order of priority:

**1** New products must appear at times which ensure that the limiting capability, whether it lies in production, development or sales, is fully loaded but not overloaded.
**2** When a choice must be made between products, the one which makes the greatest use of the company's differentiated assets should be chosen.
**3** When the first two criteria have been satisfied, the products with the best ratio of sales gross margin to development costs should be chosen. The influence of time should be assessed by discounting future income at a severe rate: say thirty per cent a year.

There is never likely to be a single solution. What is necessary is to accept the constraints which the total situation imposes, take the overall business strategy—technical, marketing, sales, manufacturing or traditional—that the company wishes to pursue, and within it work out the best new product plan possible.

### 3:14   Departmental strength and business strategy

We have dealt with the five principal new product strategies by which a company that develops a new product may hope to attract customers. Each requires a different emphasis in its technical, commercial and manufacturing departments. Consider them in turn under the same headings.

*Technical leadership.* The product is intended to sell because it does something better than anything else available. This usually results from some novel technique or material, which is likely to have emerged from a research laboratory. The obvious inference is that a strong research department is an essential base for a technical strategy. Development and design must play their part and the essential point is that they must be fast. The selling point of the product is to be that it is unique. It is unlikely to enjoy this advantage for long and it is necessary to exploit the advantage while it lasts. Economy in production, elegance in design and all the other things that make or mar most products are secondary to the fact of existence, and all efforts must be concentrated on getting the product onto the market without delay.

Good marketing information is essential. Scientists notoriously want to make anything that is novel or ingenious, regardless of its real appeal to customers. Some of them even concentrate on particular areas of technology, disregarding all others. The research laboratories should be expected to propose new products but it is the marketing department which should assess their potential. It must base this not only on customers needs but also on the probable developments in other technologies.

Sales and production are much less important. Provided they are reasonably effective they will suffice. If the company has any special skills in these areas it will do better to concentrate them on products which have no intrinsic advantages.

*Market conditions.* Just as a technical strategy requires a good marketing department, a marketing strategy requires a good research laboratory. The future of any product may be affected by the changes which scientific advances make possible, and unless the marketing department has as clear a grasp of technical developments as it has of market requirements, its forecasts will not be accurate. This can only come from close contact with a research laboratory.

Development, design and production have got priorities which differ from those for technically oriented products. Speed is no longer important, for the essence of a good market prediction is that it will be made in plenty of time and that the market will last. For the same reasons there is every opportunity for quality of design and economy of production. Although sales may still be made without these advantages, profitability and reputation depend on them.

Selling is not a major factor in the success of a market oriented product. If the prediction is good and demand is ahead of productive capacity, salesmen will spend more time making excuses for poor deliveries than in seeking new orders. Even this calls for some skill, but it falls far short of that required to sell in a genuinely competitive situation.

*Manufacturing advantages.* A product chosen because it can be manufactured more economically than those of competitors is unlikely to depend on the work of a research laboratory or even to require much development. What it does need is a first class design team closely integrated with the production department.

The need for a good production department is obvious, but it is not always clear how dependent this is on marketing forecasts. The cheapest way to make anything depends on the numbers to be made. The reasons for this have been discussed in paragraph 3:9 and here it need only be pointed out that the marketing department must establish the vital equations connecting price and sales volume. It is on this that the choice of manufacturing techniques depends.

The sales department has a part to play but it is not of major importance. If the product is really cheaper than its competitors there is no real selling to be done. All that is necessary is to visit customers, show them the goods, and book their orders.

*Salesman's advice.* The decision to base a new product on the ability of the sales department requires careful thought. It accepts that the product will have no technical advantages over those of competitors, that it will not be cheaper, that it will not go into a market that lacks other sources of supply and that its success depends entirely on the activity and resourcefulness of the sales team.

It is clear that if this strategy is adopted research and marketing have only the minor role of giving warning of any developments that are likely to make the product obsolete. Development and production must be reasonably efficient but they need not be outstanding. Their task is to do as well as those of competitors. The extra edge is to come from the sales force. The important thing to ensure is that this strategy is chosen only for products in which it can succeed. If they are of a type in which a better research effort or a more highly mechanised production capability will yield dividends, they should not be selected. The best sales force can do little if it has inferior goods or higher prices to contend with. It is when there are no technical advantages and when well established methods cannot be bettered that sales effort can turn the scales.

*Habit and tradition.* There is no more powerful nor more dangerous asset than tradition. Although there are people who crave for change and variety, there are many more who will stick to the same tailor, tobacco, television programme or anything else so long as it gives them reasonable satisfaction. Such customers are the backbone of every business and they must be cultivated carefully. The essential thing is to understand why they are satisfied.

If it is technical novelty, the research department must be kept up to the mark. If it is low cost, production must not lag in its methods. If it is the attention of salesmen, they must not slacken their efforts. In every case there will be a time interval between any deterioration in the vital service and the loss of custom and therein lies the danger. If the vital point is not recognised and kept under pressure, performance will not be maintained. By the time that sales start to fall the damage will be too serious to cure quickly.

A strategy based on retaining traditional customers can be outstandingly successful, but it must be based on a continuing asset.

### 3:15   The nature of product planning decisions

In the long term a company can be successful only if the right product planning decisions are made at the right time. This makes it essential that the process of decision making is clearly defined and that the vital difference between policy and executive decisions is appreciated.

*Methods of deciding policy.* Industrial history abounds with tales of men of genius who have single handedly piloted great companies to success. Many of these accounts spring from cases in which men have seen new opportunities, have grasped them, and have founded businesses on them. This can still happen but it is not a significant factor in the activities of the times in which we live. The environment is so complicated, the opportunities are hedged in by such varied difficulties and so many people are fighting over the same ground, that it is usually beyond the ability of any individual to collect for himself all the information on which decisions must be based. The best that he can do is to examine the facts brought together by marketing, technical and other specialists and to test them by questioning and arguments. He becomes an integrator and co-ordinator rather than an originator.

In practice the process of testing and examining the information assembled by specialists is far better performed by a group of people of varied outlook and experience. The best man, on his own, will make gross mistakes, but the likelihood of a serious flaw in recommendations of the specialists escaping the notice of a whole group who have shared an active discussion, is quite small. This leads to the normal method of making policy decisions. The facts are assembled by experts who also make recommendations, sometimes suggesting alternatives. They are discussed in open forum by senior executives and in the great majority of cases the best course of action emerges. Occasionally different opinions remain, and in this case either a vote or the decision of a particular individual settles which line is to be followed. Once the decision is made the duties of the policy making body are at an end. Open discussion is the way to decide policy: entirely different methods are required when it has to be implemented.

*Implementing the policy decisions.* In implementation of policy there is no longer any question of whether something is to be done. The only issue is how it is to be done. Here, too, no single individual can know enough to settle everything. A chain of commands must go all the way from the board room to the work bench, and at every stage the man who gives an instruction should take full advantage of the special knowledge of the next man in the chain. He can do this by stating what is to be achieved and then discussing the best way of achieving it or the nearest approach to it that is possible.

There is no reason why a planner should not be an executive or an executive a planner. The secret of efficiency is that he should fulfil one function at a time and that he should not confuse them. He should bear in mind these steps in the appearance of a new product:

**1** The facts on which new product decisions are to be made are assembled by specialists.
**2** The implications of these facts are debated by a senior and representative body and decisions made. These will usually be unanimous but some mechanism for resolving differences is necessary.

This completes the decision making process and implementation follows:

**1** The executives responsible for new product development prepare plans to implement these decisions.
**2** These plans are tested by discussion of each step with the men who will have to carry it out and where necessary the plans are modified to make the best use of available resources.

### 3:16 Formal planning process

Decisions are not made by individuals: they emerge from discussion. Paradoxically, responsibility must lie with individuals. Their responsibility is to see that the right people discuss the right questions at the right time, that they make decisions where decisions are required, and that a proper chain of authority for implementation is set up. The whole planning process can be outlined in terms of these individuals and groups and the things that they have to do.

*Role of the product planner.* In every product area one man should have responsibility for product planning. This may be a full-time or a part-time commitment. He must be in close touch with every department of his company and with their assistance he must assemble the following information:

**1** The history and predicted future of each existing product. This is the basis of the chart shown in Figure 3:1.
**2** The status of each product under development and its predicted future sales. The status may usefully be shown on a chart like that of Figure 3:2. The future sales will be included in Figure 3:1.
**3** The possible future products foreseen by research, and what can be predicted of their development and sales cycles.
**4** The future products required by marketing together with estimates of development and sales cycles.
**5** Any product proposals from other parts of the company.

*The planning committee.* This committee has the future of the business in its hands and its calibre is crucial. The chairman should be a very

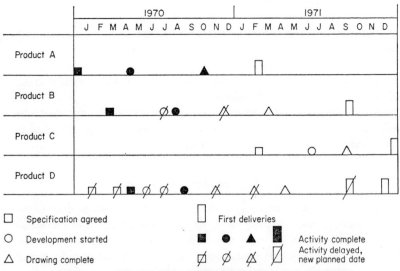

FIGURE 3:2   PRODUCT DEVELOPMENT PROGRESS
CHART
Marked up to December 1970

senior executive. In a business with a small number of separate products, he will probably be the managing director. In a business with many products the position is more likely to be delegated to a divisional manager or to a member of the functional staff.

The members of the committee will include at least one representative from each of the commercial, technical, financial and manufacturing functions of the division that is to produce the products. They will be assisted by the best talent available from functional staff. The product planner will prepare the agenda for the committee. He should be encouraged to stick his neck out by making positive recommendations. The stages through which the committee should work are:

**1** Establish on the basis of the predicted sales of existing products and the capacity, present or future, of the departments concerned, what level of new products can be handled.
**2** Consider the proposals collected by the planner and allocate priorities on the basis of use of company assets as indicated in section 3 : 5.
**3** Compare the demands on research and development resources of the products with those available.
**4** Attempt to find a solution that will maintain a full load on the limiting resource, using products of the highest priority, without overstraining other parts of the organisation.

*Developmental management.* The development manager will be a member of the planning committee and as such will take part in the debate and decisions. When he leaves the meeting his role changes. His duty is to carry out what has been decided, not to question it any further. In doing so he should be guided by the principle of concentration of resources in development. This can be illustrated by the case in which ten men are available and two products are to be developed, each requiring ten man-years of effort. If they are done in parallel both will complete simultaneously in two years' time. If the first is tackled by the whole team it will complete in the first year and the second will be completed in the second year. Thus twelve months will have been gained on one product without anything having been lost on the second.

There are obvious limitations in this over-simplified approach but the principle is a sound one. Every project should have the optimum number of men put on to it. When no more men are available the projects that are left must wait. To spread resources thinly over too many projects at one time delays those with high priority without doing anything to speed up the others.

On this basis a PERT or other similar chart is drawn up for each chosen product development. This includes laboratory experiments, prototype construction and testing, release of drawings to production, tooling and provisioning, advertising, selling, and all the other things that must be done before the product reaches its final customers. Every activity on the chart requires consultation with the men who are to carry it out, for in most cases only they know what resources they will have available and the best method of operation. There must be no doubt in anyone's mind that they are discussing *how* to do it, not *whether* to do it.

The sort of chart that emerges is shown in Figure 3:3. It is based on the milestones against which progress will be monitored and the demands that will be made upon men, money and other resources. Each department will have its own PERT charts breaking down the activities shown on the master chart of Figure 3:3 into sufficient detail to give accurate estimates and an adequate basis for monitoring of progress. It will be responsible for ensuring that the load that is described is compatible with its other commitments.

When these charts have all been completed and the commitments accepted it only remains for the development manager to report to the planning committee the key dates in his plan and for the product planning manager to enter them on his charts. Provided the committee accepts them the planning process is complete.

### 3:17   Case history

The principles which have been stated in general terms may be illustrated by considering the activities of a product planner in a hypothetical company. This company manufactures capacitors for sale to the electronic equipment industry. At the time when a plan is being prepared, these are of three types; aluminium electrolytic, tantalum electrolytic and paper dielectric.

*Production loading.* The first task of the product planner is to study the order books, discuss the sales targets and investigate the factory capacity. His conclusion, reached by questioning his colleagues and taking a view on the credibility of their answers, is that capacity will be fully loaded for six months (say to the end of 1971), that the load will fall to two thirds of this level over the following six months and that it will be down to one half by the end of 1972.

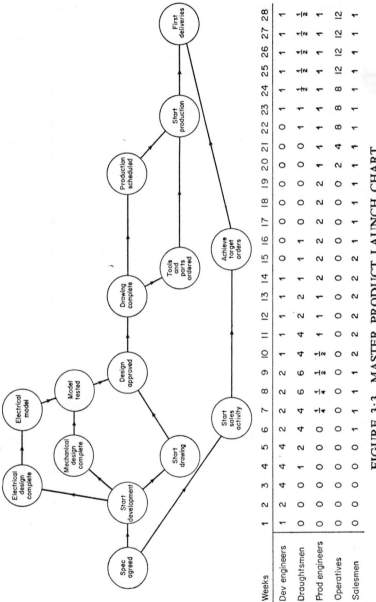

| Weeks | 1 | 2 | 3 | 4 | 5 | 6 | 7 | 8 | 9 | 10 | 11 | 12 | 13 | 14 | 15 | 16 | 17 | 18 | 19 | 20 | 21 | 22 | 23 | 24 | 25 | 26 | 27 | 28 |
|---|---|---|---|---|---|---|---|---|---|---|---|---|---|---|---|---|---|---|---|---|---|---|---|---|---|---|---|---|
| Dev engineers | 1 | 2 | 4 | 4 | 4 | 2 | 2 | 2 | 2 | 1 | 1 | 1 | 1 | 1 | 1 | 0 | 0 | 0 | 0 | 0 | 0 | 0 | 1 | 1 | 1 | 1 | 1 | 1 |
| Draughtsmen | 0 | 0 | 0 | 1 | 2 | 4 | 4 | 6 | 6 | 4 | 4 | 2 | 2 | 1 | 1 | 1 | 0 | 0 | 0 | 0 | 0 | 1 | 1 | $\frac{1}{2}$ | $\frac{1}{2}$ | $\frac{1}{2}$ | $\frac{1}{2}$ | $\frac{1}{2}$ |
| Prod engineers | 0 | 0 | 0 | 0 | 0 | 0 | $\frac{1}{4}$ | $\frac{1}{4}$ | $\frac{1}{2}$ | $\frac{1}{2}$ | 1 | 1 | 1 | 2 | 2 | 2 | 2 | 2 | 2 | 1 | 1 | 1 | 1 | 1 | 1 | 1 | 1 | 1 |
| Operatives | 0 | 0 | 0 | 0 | 0 | 0 | 0 | 0 | 0 | 0 | 0 | 0 | 0 | 0 | 0 | 0 | 0 | 0 | 0 | 2 | 4 | 8 | 8 | 8 | 12 | 12 | 12 | 12 |
| Salesmen | 0 | 0 | 0 | 0 | 0 | 1 | 1 | 1 | 1 | 2 | 2 | 2 | 2 | 2 | 2 | 2 | 1 | 1 | 1 | 1 | 1 | 1 | 1 | 1 | 1 | 1 | 1 | 1 |

FIGURE 3:3   MASTER PRODUCT LAUNCH CHART
From which each department prepares its own detailed charts

To this he will add two figures obtained by discussion with account-ants and industrial engineers. The first is that each one per cent of capacity unused would result in a loss of profit and overhead recovery at the rate of £2500 a month. The second is that to extend the factory would cost £10 000 for each £4000 worth of monthly output, and that it would take nine months from the date of the decision to the first output.

*Production profiles.* Each of the three product types has its own predicted history. The demand for aluminium electrolytics will fall as the enter-tainment market continues the move to solid state circuitry. The demand for tantalum electrolytics will grow to keep pace with the expanding sales of solid state electronic equipment. Paper dielectric capacitors will be replaced by plastic foil types.

The aluminium and paper types are sold in a competitive market, making gross margins of only 25 per cent. The tantalums are technical leaders with a clear advantage over anything else available and command a premium price which gives a 60 per cent gross margin. Consequently with only 20 per cent of the total production they provide nearly 40 per cent of the total recoveries.

All these statements depend on an analysis of information coming from sales, from marketing, from production, from engineering and from technical journals. To collect the information and to carry out the analysis are crucial parts of the planning process.

*New product suggestions.* The sales department wants a wider range of aluminium electrolytics, a new range of plastic foil capacitors and more output of tantalums.

The marketing department advises that there will soon be excess capacity in the industry for aluminium electrolytics, that the demand for plastics will grow fast and that the heavy demand for tantalums will continue. The research and development department warns that the technical lead enjoyed by the tantalums is likely to be overtaken by competitors within six months and that an improvement sufficient to restore the lead would require the efforts of at least half the staff available over this period. They suggest twelve new types of aluminium electrolytics which would widen the range and estimate that with half the total staff devoted to this task the designs could be made available to production at the rate of two a month starting in December 1971. A similar force could make the first plastic capacitors available in mid-1972 and a full range by mid-1973.

*Planning meeting.* By the time that the information given above has been collected, most of the work has been done. Of course nobody will be anxious to accept the view that the business is heading for trouble and the planner must expect a vigorous debate, but provided he convinces his colleagues of the accuracy of his information and analysis the range of choices open is severely circumscribed. It depends on three factors:

**1** Although new aluminium electrolytics could be ready in time to keep up the load on the factory, they will be entering a shrinking market and one that might contain too much manufacturing capacity. Consequently the margins will be poor.
**2** Unless half the available research and development force is set to work on tantalums, the technical lead, and with it the high profit, is likely to disappear within six months.
**3** If only half the research and development force is put onto plastics, they will be six months too late to fill the gap left by falling sales of existing types.

The right decisions are far from obvious. They might be based on acceptance of the estimates of sales or development departments or alternatively on insistence that they must do better. The vital point is that a new product cannot be considered in isolation. It is part of a complete business, depending on every department and constrained by every other product activity. It cannot be planned on its own. It can only be allocated a place in an overall business plan.

# FOUR

# Manpower Planning

*by E S M Chadwick*

As competitive pressures intensify, the need for a continuing and disciplined look at manpower problems has become increasingly clear. Most companies have become acutely aware of the problem of manpower costs, which, even in capital intensive industries, can amount to one-third or more of total operating costs. Demands for higher standards of living and increased leisure are tending to push these up at an even faster rate and staff of the quality companies need in ever-increasing numbers are difficult to recruit and retain.

Few companies apply the same level of consideration or criteria to manpower as they do to capital investment. The traditional attitude to manpower is as a cost rather than an investment, yet manpower represents the most valuable asset which a company possesses and the one on which, above all, its future prosperity depends. The objective, therefore, is to make the best use of manpower in order to ensure both their personal satisfaction and a maximum return to the company on the costs they represent.

It may be argued that, unlike machines, people are adaptable and that the needs of manpower in the future, as in the past, can be met by recruitment when the need arises. But there is ample evidence to show that for some time to come there will be a shortage of manpower, particularly of quality manpower. In addition, changes in manpower requirements in terms of skills are likely to be much more rapid in the future than they have been in the past when there was usually adequate time to make skill adjustments. No longer will a man be able to learn **a** skill in his youth which will carry him through the whole of his working life. It is probable that the young and the not so young will have to change his skill once, or even twice, during the course of his working life. One needs to anticipate these changing needs to gain the lead time necessary to adjust to them.

Not everyone agrees that there is a shortage of quality; some take the view that there is considerable under-use of existing talents and abilities; that there is a large, as yet untapped, potential for the exercise of higher skills, if only adequate training and education can be made available. This, in itself, is a very broad subject. Suffice to say here that manpower planning must go hand-in-hand with activities directed toward the optimum effective use of manpower. Indeed, this is the primary purpose of manpower planning.

## 4:1　Role and content of manpower planning

The task of manpower planning crystallises the new demands which are being made on those responsible for the management of personnel. Planning in this field has to reconcile two apparently differing strands: those concerned with the accepted managerial yardsticks of costs, trends, projections, and so on, and the more traditional staff management approach summed up as "concern for individuals." In fact, experience shows that these attitudes are not in opposition but that they complement each other. The really skilful manager is the man who is equipped to consider the immediate implication of an individual case in a company and national context in the long term. Decisions and advice given after consideration of both short and long-term factors is likely to be of more value both to the individuals who may be involved and to the management.

In its broadest sense, manpower planning can obviously cover the total activity of the personnel function—records, recruitment, selection, training and development, appraisal, career planning, management, succession and so on. But it has become increasingly clear that it is important, both for analytical purposes and ultimately for executive purposes, to disentangle these activities and to think of them as a number of sequential phases. These can be considered in various ways, but it has been found convenient to group them into three main phases:

**1** *The development of manpower objectives.* This is concerned with the development of forecasts of the manpower necessary to fulfil the company's *corporate* objectives; with looking at the totality of situations rather than at individuals. In this phase, analysis, forecasting and the setting of targets are in terms of total numbers, skill groups, organisational groups, total costs and so on. It is concerned with detailed analyses in order to identify and foresee problem areas, to assess future demands and to establish how those demands may be met. Overall, it is directed towards the development of a manpower *strategy*, linked with—in fact, an integral part of—company strategy.

**2** *Management of manpower.* In this phase, the problem is of managing manpower resources in order to meet objectives and the development in more specific and individual terms of recruitment plans, training and development plans, succession plans, appraisal systems and so on.

**3** *Control and evaluation.* The continual evaluation and amendment of plans in the light of achievement and changing circumstances.

The components of the second phase of this progression are fairly familiar and in some areas of industry are often taken to be synonymous with manpower planning. Phase 1, on the other hand, though obviously supplying the general context in which phase 2 must operate, has not yet developed the familiar practices and techniques of phase 2.

It is the ultimate aim of manpower planning that these three phases should be fully integrated (see Figure 4:1). It is equally clear that manpower planning must be fully integrated with the company plan. Indeed, without a company plan, there can be no realistic manpower planning. This chapter deals primarily with phase 1 and with the analysis of manpower and the forecasting of needs to meet the particular manpower objectives. Unless this phase of planning is well understood, the vital second phase takes on an atmosphere of uncertainty and becomes an operation concerned entirely with short-term tactics and without any particular strategy in mind. The equally vital, and again less familiar, third phase of control and evaluation is also dealt with in some detail.

Within phase 1, manpower planning in companies ranging in size from 450 employees upward has shown that whatever the differences of size and background, seven major considerations have been common to them all:

**1** The necessity for the closest co-operation between those working on manpower planning and the rest of management. Manpower planning is a total management activity.

**2** The growing importance of the cost of manpower in the day-to-day operations of every company.

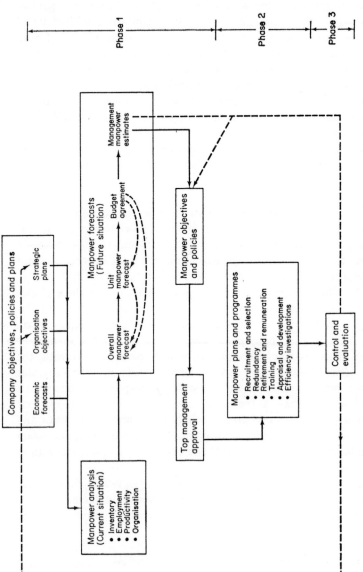

FIGURE 4:1  A PROCEDURE FOR MANPOWER PLANNING
Showing the three phases of manpower planning in their logical
sequence together with the information feedback loop which
must result from the final phase of control and evaluation

**3** The importance of manpower as an asset in the long-term operations of companies—an asset that can increase in value through careful utilisation.

**4** The difficulty of recruiting and retaining high potential personnel who are in ever-increasing demand.

**5** The rapidly changing distribution of skills available and required in each company.

**6** The importance of the social environment and the outside pressures which may bear on a company and restrict its freedom of action in the manpower field.

**7** The importance of the educational system, its output at each of its stages and the rise in the general educational standard of new recruits at every level.

### 4:2 Planning time scale

The question of how far ahead one should attempt to look can give rise to a great deal of discussion. Much depends on the particular circumstances. However, in most situations, five years is a reasonable period. Such a period covers, for example, most types of apprenticeships and, in general, gives the appropriate lead time necessary to deal with most manpower situations. An overriding factor is the period of company plans because, and this cannot be emphasised too strongly, without a company plan there can be no realistic manpower plan. There are, of course, some exceptions to the five year period. It is, for example, rarely necessary, except for broad costing forecasts, to think five years ahead for unskilled and semi-skilled categories of personnel who can be comparatively easily and quickly recruited and trained for production. Occasional operating or organisational situations can also render some aspects of the future so unpredictable that, for the time being, planning has to be very short-term; an impending major re-organisation, for example, or fluctuating events in sales or promotion policy. Nevertheless, even with such situations, the need for the development of a broad strategy remains.

It also remains that for some activities and notably some individual career development plans, five years can be a comparatively short period. Consequently, in some individual cases in areas of phase 2, a five-year planning period, though possibly only able to cover part of the plan concerning an individual, is a *practical* period for looking ahead in terms of the actual action contributing to the long-term aim.

## 4:3  Limitations of manpower planning

It is important to bear in mind what can reasonably be expected from manpower planning, and indeed of any planning. The aim is the reduction of uncertainty, but the possibility of doing this varies inversely with time. The increasingly tentative nature of these forecasts covering the later years of the planning period must, therefore, be appreciated. It may be more appropriate to think of the five-year period as comprising a two-year plan (a plan implying action) and a three-year forecast.

Manpower planning is concerned with an asset, the individual components of which do not lend themselves to precise measurement and docketing and which often behave in a quite unpredictable way. It has to deal with this asset in a trading and technical situation which is also fluid and where targets and plans have often to be radically adjusted at short notice. Consequently, the manpower planning activity shares, in a particularly acute way, the essential characteristics of all planning in an uncertain world—it is a never-ending readjustment of expectations and aims to meet changing goals within a very uncertain environment. Its language and results will therefore be probablistic in nature and will *not* be inflexible commitments to some postulated single course of events.

Above all, it is not a new and revolutionary approach to problems that have only recently been identified; indeed, many of its strands have long been common practice in many companies. The problem is to bring these practices together into a systematic approach that directs attention to the *future* and to the identification of potential manpower problems.

This chapter sets out to describe a number of possible analytical approaches which have been found to be useful. But manpower is the most unpredictable and socially conditioned section of every company's assets and there is no single universally applicable system of manpower planning. It is for each company to consider those approaches and methods which seem relevant to its own situation. The check list given in Figure 4:2 may be helpful in identifying particular needs.

## 4:4  Compiling the planning data

Experience has shown that in the first phase of manpower planning there are various elements which go to make up the total picture. The first essential is data, without which no planning is possible. Additionally, one needs to define the present position and to analyse trends,

| | ROOM FOR IMPROVE- MENT | ADEQUATE | GOOD—NO WEAKNESSES |
|---|---|---|---|
| 1 Top management and organisational support for manpower plans and programmes | | | |
| 2 An adequate information system on manpower | | | |
| 3 Anticipation of future manpower requirements | | | |
| 4 Integration of manpower programmes with overall company objectives | | | |
| 5 The anticipation of organisational changes and preparing for their manpower implications | | | |
| 6 Recruitment of necessary number of well-qualified staff at each level | | | |
| 7 Effective placement of newly engaged graduate/professional staff to make them productive | | | |
| 8 Filling key middle and top management posts with well-qualified staff | | | |
| 9 Management of age structure to minimise wastage problems and avoid promotion blockages | | | |
| 10 Reducing wastage at all levels | | | |
| 11 Providing significant jobs for managers throughout their career | | | |
| 12 Evaluating the current performance of all staff | | | |

FIGURE 4:2 MANPOWER PLANNING CHECKLIST
Designed to evaluate the effectiveness of manpower planning
in a company. The aim is to help identify those areas where
manpower management is underdeveloped and where further
planning and development are needed

| | ROOM FOR IMPROVEMENT | ADEQUATE | GOOD—NO WEAKNESSES |
|---|---|---|---|
| 13 Evaluating the potential of all staff for promotion and of managers for higher responsibilities | | | |
| 14 Providing sound promotion and career opportunities for all staff with potential | | | |
| 15 Motivating managers to develop their subordinates | | | |
| 16 Development of managers for higher level responsibilities | | | |
| 17 Keeping the remuneration system up-to-date and effective as a motivator | | | |
| 18 Investigation into the causes and solutions of serious manpower problems | | | |
| 19 Measuring productivity improvements | | | |
| 20 Maintenance of a system that enables the cost of manpower and its contribution to the company effort to be evaluated | | | |
| 21 Maintenance of a comprehensive and systematic programme of training to enable staff to adapt to new procedures and techniques and to equip them for higher responsibilities | | | |
| 22 Maintenance of a sound and flexible organisation structure | | | |
| 23 Integration of the manpower management programmes | | | |

FIG. 4.2 (*cont.*)

to consider changing company objectives and their manpower implications and, out of this, to define manpower objectives. All are necessary for the analytical and methodological framework that lies under the preparation of a plan.

In day-to-day practice these divisions into separate elements are perhaps somewhat artificial and tend to merge at various points. Nevertheless, it is useful for analytical purposes to consider them as separate, but related, issues.

*Basic individual data.* Adequate data is as fundamental to manpower planning as it is to any other area of planning. Staff data traditionally tends to be organised with the primary aim of supplying information on *individuals*; for planning purposes it is vital that such information should be organised in a manner that makes information easily available on the behaviour of groups. For the purposes of phase 1 planning, the following basic data on individuals is necessary.

| | |
|---|---|
| Name | Department location |
| Identity number | Date joined department |
| Sex | Grade salary |
| Marital status | Date entered grade |
| Date of birth | Qualifications/skills |
| Date joined company | Designation/appointment |

Assessment and potential: immediate, in five years, ultimately

In addition to this basic information, a great deal of other data is obviously necessary in order to deal with individuals and the problem of phase 2, and to meet particular statutory requirements. This is, however, the minimum information needed to analyse over time the behaviour of the various groups that go to make up a company.

*Organisation and retrieval methods.* In order to make the best use of the data outlined above, it is essential to organise it in such a way that it can be sorted and arranged to illustrate not only the present position in any group or combination of groups, but also the changes that have taken place over time and to measure the trends that become apparent.

Various means are available, from simple needle-sorting punch card systems to computers. The decision as to which to use depends on cost, facilities already available, size of company, and so on.

*Costs data.* The situation and trends that this personnel data will be used to illustrate are, of course, also reflected in financial terms and particularly in the form of costs. Much of the data concerned with this aspect of manpower will be with the accountants, but those concerned with the management of personnel will want to keep, or have ready access to, information that will give the total cost of the manpower used in the company and of the elements which go to make up the total.

This raises the question of definition and consistency in use that will need to be agreed with the accountants. Most companies see their manpower costs as falling into two main groups—those directly associated with salary and those costs which can vary with company policy and may even, for some considerations, include accommodation costs. It may be convenient to think of those costs in the following way:

| DIRECT MANPOWER COSTS | MANPOWER SERVICING COSTS |
|---|---|
| Salaries/wages | Fringe benefits: |
| | 1 Catering costs |
| Pension fund contributions and other salary associated costs | 2 Welfare and social costs |
| | Operating costs: |
| Salary-associated statutory costs, such as national insurance charges, payroll taxes | 1 Accommodation and office service costs |
| | 2 Equipment costs |
| | 3 Secretarial costs |
| | 4 Medical costs |
| | 5 Administration costs |
| | 6 Training costs |

There may be other costs within the area of servicing costs such as subsidised housing, travel and the supply or subsidising of cars, supply of clothing, and so on.

The inclusion of such costs as those of accommodation and secretarial services raise, of course, further questions of definition, because it can be argued that accommodation normally exists already. But office accommodation can be expensive and it is salutary to keep in mind the possible ultimate consequences of expanding numbers. Nor must the "opportunity cost" of using existing accommodation for purposes other than personnel be overlooked.

*National and social data.* The extent to which it is necessary to keep this data varies from company to company, but it is generally necessary to have information on such matters as:

1    Availability trends in the various levels of the labour market—national and local
2    Anticipated trends in inflation and the cost of living
3    Anticipated changes in the cost and framework of the social services
4    Changes in educational structure
5    Anticipated taxation changes affecting manpower

### 4:5 Present position and analysis of trends

It is axiomatic that the starting point of any plan (and any control system) must be a careful analysis and tabulation of the position as it exists at the start point of the planning period and in terms of the manpower already employed.

This information is needed in a series of permutations according to the precise needs of the company. Its retrievability and easy collation is the test of the efficiency of any data system.

*Direct manpower.* The following are the basic "building-blocks" that are needed in most circumstances:
1    Present total manpower
2    Manpower resources by appropriate planning groups, such as:
   (*a*)  Sex
   (*b*)  Grade
   (*c*)  Function/department
   (*d*)  Profession/skill
   (*e*)  Qualification
   (*f*)  Age group
   (*g*)  Length of service

3    Total costs
4    Total costs by appropriate component elements, such as salaries, wages, pension contributions, welfare, canteen, and so on
5    Costs by functions/departments
6    Costs indices and ratios (see phase 3—Control and Evaluation—page 124)
7    Total numbers related to sales, production, or such other criteria as may be appropriate, in physical and financial terms

8    Attrition and retention rates by appropriate groups, that
     is, overall, by function/department, by profession, by sex,
     by age group, and so on
9    Recruitment patterns by age, education, for each depart-
     ment
10   Resources of promotable staff

*Present organisation and manpower policies.* The manpower pattern
revealed by these analyses will be operating in a specific context and
either explicitly or implicitly the manpower plan has to keep this context in mind. Obviously a large number of subtle pressures will be at
work and these pressures will vary from company to company. Many
of them are not normally of immediate day-to-day concern to those
responsible for manpower planning and management, but they under-
line how important it is for such people to keep themselves in the general
management picture. Among the questions to be borne in mind are:

1    National and market considerations
  (*a*) The general position of the company in relation to
       national policies, both economic and social
  (*b*) The company's market share in relation to other com-
       panies
  (*c*) The position in the labour market for the various cate-
       gories employed
2    Company considerations
  (*a*) The present personnel policies and practices of the
       company including policy towards manpower costs,
       working hours, holidays, and so on
  (*b*) Manning schedules of offices, factories, depots, on the
       basis of the present organisation
  (*c*) Volume (expressed in appropriate units) and ranges of
       products being handled
  (*d*) Present sales or production objectives
  (*e*) Present supply and distribution pattern
  (*f*) Present state of the various technologies employed by the
       company

*Collation of information and identification of trends.* Various methods of
organising, displaying and comparing this data have been developed
in order to show the present manpower position and the trends that
have developed. Some examples are listed here as general illustrations;
these can be adjusted to meet any particular need.

**1** *Organisation*

(*a*) General organisation showing distribution of departments and numbers by categories.

(*b*) Series of detailed organigrams of individual departments showing name, job title and grade of individuals or small groups of individuals.

(*c*) Some system of staff classification, for example:

| | | |
|---|---|---|
| *A* | Management | |
| | Top Grade | } Senior management |
| | Grade 1 | |
| *B* | Senior staff | |
| | Grade 2 | |
| | Grade 3 | |
| | Grade 4 | } Work of a graduate/professional level |
| | Grade 5 | |
| *C* | Junior staff | |
| | Grade 6 | |
| | Grade 7 | |
| | Grade 8 | } Technical assistants, clerical staff |
| | Grade 9 | |
| *D* | Craftsmen and labourers | |
| | Grade 10 | Craftsmen |
| | Grade 11 | Semi-skilled |
| | Grade 12 | Unskilled |

This is intended only as an illustration, the classification would naturally be related to the detailed system actually used by a company. But some such classification is necessary as an aid to general understanding and as a help in considering sources of promotion potential.

(*d*) The development of the organisation over the previous five years

**2** *Strengths, wastage, recruitment and age structures*

(*a*) Tabular and/or graphical illustrations of changes in total, functional and departmental grade strengths to date and comparative changes in strengths. Anticipated changes can also be included as illustrated in the next section.

(*b*) Current strengths by age and anticipated effect of wastage on recruitment. Age structure histograms are usually constructed in five-year bands. The groups, especially in larger companies, should be carefully defined, because different factors affect different groups. Age structures of total employees would, for example, have little meaning. This method of analysis can be extended as is discussed on page 118.

(*c*) Strengths by age and grade groups and trends in grade group distribution.

(*d*) Changes in the educational background of the company's employees.

(*e*) The promotion potential within the company.

### 3  *Staff costs*
(*a*) Total salary and manpower costs, revenue costs, sales revenue and so on.

(*b*) Development of components of total costs.

(*c*) Total costs overall and by functions and departments.

(*d*) Trends in salary/wage levels and total salary/wage costs.

### 4:6  Company objectives and their manpower implications

Having established the present position in all its aspects on the lines that have been discussed, it then becomes necessary to consider what changes from that position are anticipated over the planning period. The knowledge of what impending changes will affect manpower is, of course, widely dispersed throughout a company and only in the smallest companies is all the knowledge likely to be held by one man. Certainly, it is unlikely that the personnel manager would have such knowledge. *The closest contact is, therefore, essential between those responsible for manpower planning and every other area of management.*

*Changes in company objectives and policies.* This is the key area to be interpreted in manpower terms. Reference has already been made to the uncertainty which makes it difficult for managers to be confident in their assessment of the manpower changes that company plans and objectives will make necessary. Nevertheless, it is vital to obtain an informed view of the future even when acknowledging that circumstances can change and that this view will become less concrete as the time-span of the forecast increases. One must compare this with the alternative, which is to drift aimlessly. Moreover, continual control and evaluation does much to offset this.

It would not be possible to list here all the possible areas which might be subject to change but the following should be considered:

1      Expansion/contraction plans for installations/factories/departments, and so on.

2      Changes in production/sales targets

3      The possible introduction of new products

4      Any projected diversification plans

5      Any anticipated organisarional change—centralisation, decentralisation, nationalisation, the implementation of organisation atnd method studies

6      Any overall budgetary constraints or targets

7      Anticipated changes in personnel policy

8      Anticipated increases in productivity

*Anticipated technological changes.* Technological changes rarely arise without warning. It is important, therefore, to keep in touch with technical developments and their manpower implications. Among these may be:

1      Automation/mechanisation of processes and procedures. In some cases work study and organisation and methods will be able to make fairly accurate forecasts of the manpower implications of changes that are at the planning stage

2      Technological evolution—improvements in present methods

3      Changes in management techniques

4      Changes in working methods and in the organisation of work—use of contracting out, consultants, and so on

*Social and economic change.* This is a very wide area covering the whole range of environmental influences bearing upon manpower. While they are outside the control of any individual company, an understanding of them and their likely impact over the planning period is essential. Among the factors that have to be considered are:

1      Trends in the cost of manpower of all types and their future implications

2      Changes in hours of work and length of holidays

3      Outputs at each level from the educational system

4      The competitive position of the company at each level of the labour market

5      Future negotiations with trades unions and developments in collective agreements

6      National policies in the labour market—redundancy legislation, taxation policy, retirement policies, and so on

7      Emigration/immigration policies

8      In some particular cases of expansion into new areas, the availability of housing and social amenities

*Secular changes within the company.* These changes are generated not by policy decisions but mainly by the demographic characteristics of the company. They include:

1    Developments within the age structure
2    Retirements
3    Promotions

### 4:7   Preparing managerial manpower forecasts (phase 1)

All the considerations which have been outlined have to be translated for manpower planning purposes into numbers. The impact of anticipated change on the present position produces the outlines of the anticipated future. A regular system is necessary (at various levels of formality) whereby the impact of change on present manpower strengths and establishments is forecast by the management concerned. The central role of the manpower planner, be it the staff manager or some other designated person, is to carry out the following:

1    Organise on a regular and consistent basis such a fore-
     casting exercise
2    Collate the resulting figures and adjust them for retire-
     ment, wastage and promotion
3    Produce agreed and authorised recruiting, training and
     promotion targets together with their cost implications

The extent to which objectives can be converted into reasonably accurate manpower figures will vary with the situation concerned. Some production and distribution situations where new facilities are involved can often be translated into specific manpower needs. Similarly, some clerical situations may also produce firm figures. Other situations, especially those which cannot be based on some measurements of production, such as head offices, must rely more on managerial forecasting and the analysis of trends.

*Method of collation.* Possible approaches to the first stage of this collating exercise are illustrated in Figure 4:3. This shows a method which has been employed to collect data in a consistent manner. It will be seen that managerial participation is the essential element. In some circumstances, this approach has also been valuable in supporting a system of establishment control and budgeting.

Estimates of staff numbers 1970—5

Functional sector_____

Department_____

| Categories of staff | Actual number at time of estimate | Expected at year end 1970 | Increases and decreases in requirements and year end balances | | | | | | | | | | | | | | |
|---|---|---|---|---|---|---|---|---|---|---|---|---|---|---|---|---|---|
| | | | Estimate | | | | | | Forecast | | | | | | | | |
| | | | 1971 | | | 1972 | | | 1973 | | | 1974 | | | 1975 | | |
| | | | − | + | = | − | + | = | − | + | = | − | + | = | − | + | = |
| | | | | | | | | | | | | | | | | | |
| Totals | | | | | | | | | | | | | | | | | |

Brief statement of reasons for increases and/or decreases.:

Signed_____ Date_____
Departmental Manager

Signed_____ Date_____
General Manager

## FIGURE 4:3  METHOD OF COLLECTING INFORMATION ON ANTICIPATED MANPOWER CHANGES

*Summarising the manpower forecast.* An example of the sort of summary that might emerge from the collation of information so gathered is given in Figure 4:4. This would, of course, be backed up by a statement giving the reasons for the various changes forecast. The picture so presented is by no means unique and illustrates the very marked changes that can take place within a numerically stable manpower situation. The wastage estimates alone represent major changes in the composition

| | Estimate | | | Forecasts | | | Totals |
|---|---|---|---|---|---|---|---|
| XYZ Manufacturing Co Ltd<br>Summary of Manpower Forecasts, 1970–5 | | | | | | | |
| | 1970 | 1971 | 1972 | 1973 | 1974 | 1975 | |
| 1  Number of jobs at<br>   1 January | 562* | 550 | 557 | 584 | 580 | 573 | — |
| 2  Anticipated changes + | 4 | 13 | 42 | 23 | 8 | 8 | + 98 |
|    in numbers and<br>    categories          − | 16 | 6 | 15 | 27 | 15 | 6 | − 85 |
| 3  Number of jobs at<br>   31 December | 550 | 557 | 584 | 580 | 573 | 575 | — |
| 4  Anticipated net<br>   changes in numbers<br>   of jobs | −12 | +7 | +27 | −4 | −7 | +2 | + 13 |
| 5  Wastage replacements<br>   required | 19 | 39 | 42 | 36 | 54 | 37 | 227 |

FIGURE 4:4   OVERALL SUMMARY OF A FIVE-YEAR
MANPOWER ESTIMATE AND FORECAST

of the work force, and, in consequence, indicate a considerable recruiting and training effort if present numbers and efficiency are to be maintained. It should be noted that ninety-eight new jobs are likely to be required but eighty-five existing jobs will disappear. It does not, or need not, follow that eighty-five employees will have to be dismissed. Wastage will undoubtedly take care of part of this problem, and the lead time gained by this exercise should enable others to be re-trained for the new tasks required. The chain of considerations involved in the collation of forecasts and, *inter alia*, the production of recruitment targets, is set out in Figure 4:5. The involvement of all management in this activity will again be noted.

## 4:8   Preparing projections of manpower trends

Simple numerical techniques can also be employed to enable projections to be made of steadily developing situations. These must be treated with caution, but are a great advance on merely awaiting events and add greatly to an understanding of what is happening within a group under study.

These projections are not an alternative to managerial manpower forecasting such as has been described in the preceding section but are

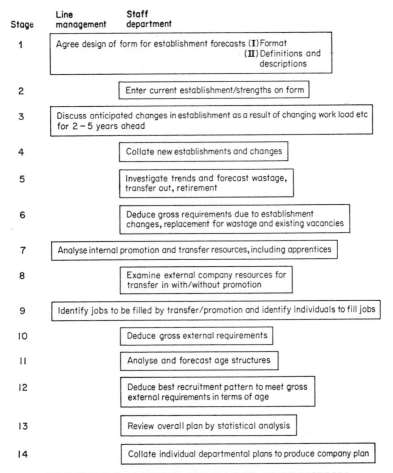

| Stage | Line management | Staff department |
|---|---|---|
| 1 | Agree design of form for establishment forecasts (**I**) Format (**II**) Definitions and descriptions | |
| 2 | Enter current establishment/strengths on form | |
| 3 | Discuss anticipated changes in establishment as a result of changing work load etc for 2 – 5 years ahead | |
| 4 | Collate new establishments and changes | |
| 5 | Investigate trends and forecast wastage, transfer out, retirement | |
| 6 | Deduce gross requirements due to establishment changes, replacement for wastage and existing vacancies | |
| 7 | Analyse internal promotion and transfer resources, including apprentices | |
| 8 | Examine external company resources for transfer in with/without promotion | |
| 9 | Identify jobs to be filled by transfer/promotion and identify individuals to fill jobs | |
| 10 | Deduce gross external requirements | |
| 11 | Analyse and forecast age structures | |
| 12 | Deduce best recruitment pattern to meet gross external requirements in terms of age | |
| 13 | Review overall plan by statistical analysis | |
| 14 | Collate individual departmental plans to produce company plan | |

FIGURE 4:5  ACTION CHAIN FOR PRODUCTION
OF RECRUITMENT TARGETS

supplementary to it. It is generally only applicable in larger companies—though the approach, if not the mathematics, can be used even in smaller companies. The basic principle is that while individuals will act and react as individuals, there are discernible patterns of behaviour in groups providing they are sufficiently large—probably not less than 100—to avoid wide fluctuations by reason of unusual individual behaviour.

The group must also be homogeneous. For example, a group of professional engineers employed on a variety of functions—development, research, maintenance and administration, let us say, and aged from 25–58 could not be considered as homogeneous, whereas a group of such engineers all employed on production and aged 25–30 could be. What constitutes homogeneity can vary somewhat from organisation to organisation and it is for those concerned to define it for themselves from their own knowledge.

*Use of historical data*. Reference has already been made to the importance of data. For the purpose of projections, the basic need is for a bank of historical data over a minimum of five years. From such a store of information, it is possible to extract such essential factors as turnover rates in whatever category is required, movements within or between categories, the probability of promotion between grades as related to age, length of service and qualifications. By this means one is able to gain insights into the understanding of situations and the relationships which brought them about; to isolate problem areas, present or future, and decide on the action needed for their solution. By establishing this picture of movements within the staff of a company, it also becomes possible to consider forecasts of movements within the next five years, to assist in policy decisions, by indicating the probable future consequences in alternative courses of action.

There is, of course, no method of establishing a staff position which, in five years' time, will *inevitably* be achieved. Decisions can, however, be made which will in all probability approximate to that position—the accuracy of the approximation depending not only on the predicting method but also on the unpredictable effect of outside influences. The aim is to examine a variety of trends and see whether the projected position achieved by these trends is satisfactory or not. The *executive decision* lies in deciding what position is desirable, what trend produces this position, and what action, if any, is necessary in order to produce that trend.

*Projection of age structures*. The analysis and projection of age structures has been found to be of particular value in the development of recruitment policies. Figure 4:6 is an example of such an analysis. In this instance, the group is career staff, defined as staff currently holding managerial or professional specialist posts or whose qualifications are such that they are potential holders of such posts. Figure 4:6a shows the existing age structure expressed in five-year bands. The bulge in the 35–45 bands which is counter-balanced by the low numbers in the under 30 and over 50 bands should be noted. The future consequences of such a situation are demonstrated in Figures 4:6b and 4:6c which show, on the basis of present wastage trends, how many of the existing staff will still be in the employment of the company five and ten years ahead and their age groupings then.

The long-term problem posed by such a structure is obvious. Figure 4:6*d* depicts a desirable age structure for this group, that is, one that with present wastage trends continuing and planned recruitment in the appropriate age groups (in this case mainly in the under 30 bands but with some in the 30–39 bands) is self-perpetuating and avoids violent upheavals arising from large numbers of staff due for retirement at the same time, and from the promotion blockages that might otherwise occur and which are certainly present in the existing situation. Figure 4:6*e* then compares this desirable structure with the existing to indicate the surpluses and shortages in the various bands.

*Assessing shortages and surpluses.* This example does not purport to represent the actual position in any particular company but it is based on actual situations which are all too common. They arise, in part, from the wide range of wastage rates between the various age groups. These may, of course, vary considerably from company to company, but with graduate/professional levels of staff such as these, turnover rates can vary considerably with age and can be of the order of ten to fifteen per cent to 30 years of age, eight to ten per cent for 30–35, and then drop fairly sharply until from 40 years on it is insignificant at one per cent or less. From 55 on it turns upward again as retirement takes effect. This poses considerable problems in the maintenance of a stable age structure and in the development of realistic career plans.

The shortage in the over 50 group in this example will resolve itself in five years but the problem of the bulge in the middle age groups will remain and will become more acute with time. It would be unrealistic to suggest that this can be resolved by any simple means. The declaration of a redundancy to dispense with the services of men for no other reason than their age is unthinkable. Nevertheless, every endeavour should be made to reduce these numbers. One way may be to encourage those whose work is not of a good standard, or who have failed to keep up with changing needs, to seek employment elsewhere with suitable compensation being given. Any such action can be spread over up to five years and need not, therefore, involve any major upheaval.

*Dealing with shortages of potential managers.* The marked shortage of under thirty-fives and particularly of under thirties will be reflected, unless remedial action is taken, in a serious shortage of senior managers

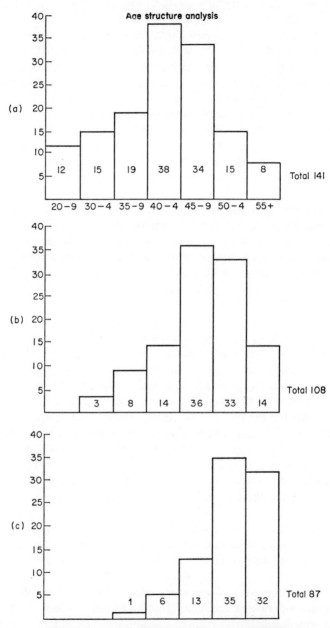

FIG. 4.6   AGE STRUCTURE ANALYSIS

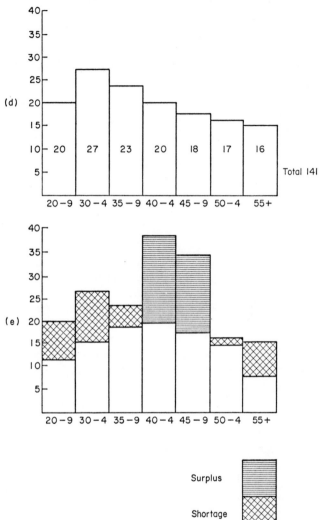

FIGURE 4:6  AGE STRUCTURE ANALYSIS
(*a*)  Present age structure
(*b*)  Numbers of present staff likely to be employed in five years
(*c*)  Numbers of present staff likely to be employed in ten years
(*d*)  Desirable age structure, based on present numbers and wastage trends
(*e*)  Present age structure compared with the desirable

| Age now | Numbers with ultimate potential to DM level — including existing DMs | Numbers available in future | | |
|---|---|---|---|---|
| | | In 5 years | In 10 years | In 15 years |
| 55+ | 2* | | | |
| 50 — 54 | 3* | 3* | | |
| 45 — 49 | 3 (1*) | 3 (1*) | | |
| 40 — 44 | 4 | 4 | 4 | |
| 35 — 39 | 3 | | 3 | 3 |
| 30 — 34 | 2 | | | 2 |
| Totals | | 10 | 7 | 5 |
| Requirements | | 6 | 6 | 6 |
| Surplus/deficit | | + 4 | + 1 | −1 |

FIGURE 4:7   ANALYSIS OF FUTURE SUPPLY OF
DEPARTMENTAL MANAGERS
On the basis of current assessment of ultimate potential
(*Existing holders of these posts)

in the future. This is demonstrated in the example given in Figure 4:7. This examines the future position for departmental managers—six in number—and, therefore, introduces a further parameter, namely, that of potential. In this analysis, a number of assumptions have been made:

1    The present policy of retirement at 60 will continue.
2    The number of such posts (though not necessarily the content) will remain unchanged.
3    No consideration has been taken of staff who are not currently identified as having potential to reach this level.

In the future, should these assumptions prove to be incorrect, proportional adjustments can be made. To this end, such an analysis should be repeated every two years.

In assessing future numbers, it has been taken that men would generally reach this level between 40 and 50 years of age.

While, in this example, the position up to five years ahead appears to be satisfactory, the longer-term outlook is a matter for concern. Bearing in mind the reserve with which assessments of long-term potential must be treated, and the incidence of wastage in the lower age groups, one would wish to have much greater potential cover. For fifteen years ahead, twice the number actually required would not be unreasonable. There is a need shown here to recruit a number of able men with potential in the under 35 group if the *future* requirements of the company are to be met.

It should be emphasised that studies such as this and others that have been described are not concerned with the present operations of a company but its ability to continue to operate efficiently in the future.

## 4:9 Management of manpower (phase 2)

In phase 2 we are concerned with the management of manpower in terms of group and individual planning in order to achieve the strategic objectives that emerge from phase 1. This area of planning is already familiar and well-developed in many companies. The subject of training and management development is dealt with at length in chapter 5. Nevertheless, in order to complete this picture of the total planning operation, it may be useful to include here a brief review of the various issues involved.

*Recruitment and selection.* The forecasts of anticipated needs that develop from collating managerial forecasts of necessary changes in establishment strengths and applying appropriate wastage factors produce a recruitment target. To attain this target a recruiting plan becomes necessary. The details and complexity of such a plan obviously vary from company to company, but include:

1  How far needs can be met from internal sources
2  The sources of outside recruitment to be approached
3  Any necessary advertising
4  The timing of recruiting
5  The selection standards to be set in any particular case

Where the plan is designed to cover five years head, it is generally preferable (in situations where highly qualified personnel are being recruited from colleges and universities) to maintain, so far as is possible, a regular annual recruitment pattern. This involves a policy of recruiting such new staff into some non-departmental status in the first instance.

*Preliminary placement.* The type of recruitment mentioned above calls for a policy covering the appropriate first placement of new recruits and the early assignments of potential managerial staff needs careful consideration. Allied to this is the general problem of turnover and the plan should have current wastage rates in mind, whether or not these are acceptable, and, if not, what corrective action is planned.

*Appraisal programmes.* The programme for the identification and appraisal of talent within the company and any anticipated changes in approach should be included.

*Development programmes.* Development programmes, covering transfers, planned rotations, promotion and training, either in terms of groups or individuals, should be dealt with.

*Retirements.* Expected retirements and consequent replacement action should be specified. Any particular action in the field of retirement administration should also be considered, such as any action necessary to either accelerate or delay particular retirements.

*Redundancy.* Any programme that may be necessary to deal with redundancies arising from reorganisation, contraction, changing needs, and so on. It is to be expected that, with proper planning, the possibility of a redundancy situation arising can be reduced. It would be naive to think that it could be entirely eliminated.

*Training.* The plan should include any broad training programmes to cover apprentice training, induction training, job training (in the widest sense) and development training which may be indicated.

*Remuneration policy.* Policy on remuneration should be dealt with not only as a matter of cost, but also as an aspect of broad motivational policy.

*Anticipated manpower investigations.* The plan should naturally include mention of any investigations into the use of manpower that may be under consideration or currently being undertaken, such as organisation and methods studies.

## 4:10   Control and evaluation (phase 3)

In the final phase of the manpower planning cycle, two broad and complementary approaches to the control and audit of the manpower plan are necessary, one in terms of numerical trends and the other in terms of costs and costs criteria.

*Numerical trends.* Fundamentally, this involves the use of controls and gauges, many of which have been in use for years. Most of these techniques are, of course, only mechanisms that show trends or divergences from the goals and expectations that have gone to make up the plan; they do not themselves *set* any goals or standards.

A great deal of control information of this type has already been mentioned earlier, but may usefully be mentioned again:

1    Changes in numbers—by total/by function/by department
2    Changes in wastage rates and reasons for wastage—in total/by department/by category/by age group, and so on
3    Changes in total costs and by their components—overall/by department/by function
4    Changing age structures and their implications
5    Developments in the educational structure of the company

More specifically, management will want to question the degree to which the various specific goals of the manpower plan were achieved.

*Costs and cost ratio approach.* This is a more "broad-brush" approach and concentrates largely on costs, both to give a comparative picture of the contribution being made by personnel to the operation of the company and to illustrate changes *within* manpower costs themselves.

The concept of productivity is very complex in practice and raises considerable theoretical problems of definition and data. Nevertheless, it has been found useful to develop a number of comparatively simple indices to illustrate the changing contribution and costs of manpower. Similarly, within the personnel function itself, ratios can be used to highlight the nature of changes within manpower costs and the impact in financial terms of specific manpower policies.

The components which go to make up manpower costs have been discussed earlier. It is a matter for individual decision as to whether all or part of these are included in considering staff expenditure. Certainly, all those costs which are directly tied to the employment of a man, such as pensions, National Health Insurance, payroll tax, and so on, should be included. A realisation of the real cost of manpower as distinct from salaries and wages can be quite salutary.

The indices that may be found to be useful will vary from company to company, depending on the nature of its activities, but some examples are:

1    $\dfrac{\text{Staff expenditure}}{\text{Average total staff numbers}}$     (*Per capita* staff costs)

2    $\dfrac{\text{Staff expenditure}}{\text{Tonnage or number of units (sales or production)}}$

3    $\dfrac{\text{Staff expenditure}}{\text{Turnover}}$

4    $\dfrac{\text{Staff expenditure}}{\text{Total operating cost}}$

Staff numbers and staff expenditure may refer to the total organisation or to any part thereof. They are best presented either graphically or in tabular form (Figure 4:8) and trends are more clearly observed if a base date is selected, represented by 100. They may go backwards in time to show past trends, or forwards to indicate the cost consequences of manpower forecasts.

Such indices must be treated with caution. Reliance on a single index could be misleading but, nevertheless, taken together, they can give an indication of trends and the movement of manpower costs related to company activities as a whole.

| Year | 1970 | 1971 | 1972 | 1973 | 1974 | 1975 |
|---|---|---|---|---|---|---|
| Sales index – units | 100 | | | | | |
| Sales proceeds index | 100 | | | | | |
| Production index | 100 | | | | | |
| Staff expenditure/ average total staff | 100 | | | | | |
| Staff expenditure/ number of sales or production units | 100 | | | | | |
| Staff expenditure/ turnover | 100 | | | | | |
| Staff expenditure/ total operating cost | 100 | | | | | |

FIGURE 4:8   SALES, PRODUCTION AND STAFF
EXPENDITURE INDICES

It is worth exploring in more detail the trends at work *within* the total costs of manpower and the operation of personnel policies. The following are suggested as ratios which help to do this but, again, they will not be applicable in every situation and will probably need adjustment to any particular circumstance:

1    Direct manpower costs

(*a*)  $\dfrac{\text{Direct manpower costs}}{\text{Turnover}}$

(*b*)  $\dfrac{\text{Direct cost of any category of employees}}{\text{Total direct manpower costs}}$

(*c*)  $\dfrac{\text{Statutory employment costs}}{\text{Direct manpower costs}}$

(*d*)  $\dfrac{\text{Pension fund, fringe benefit costs}}{\text{Direct manpower costs}}$

2    Manpower servicing costs

(*a*)  $\dfrac{\text{Manpower servicing costs}}{\text{Total manpower costs}}$

(*b*)  $\dfrac{\text{Manpower servicing costs}}{\text{Turnover}}$

(*c*)  $\dfrac{\text{Training costs}}{\text{Direct manpower costs}}$

(*d*)  $\dfrac{\text{Catering cost}}{\text{Total number of employees}}$

Other indices may include any one of the components of direct or manpower servicing costs as a proportion of the total turnover or total number of employees.

## 4:11   Summary and conclusion

The need to plan manpower as one does other resources has only recently been recognised, yet it is true to say that the prosperity and growth of any company rests, in the end, on the quality of its manpower and the extent to which its talents and abilities are utilised to the full.

By the study, analysis and planning of manpower, it becomes possible to isolate problem areas, present and future, and to take action for their solution, to decide upon action which, while meeting present needs will, at the same time, safeguard the future and not merely create further problems. It will help to avoid the loss of opportunities through lack of the appropriate manpower and the wastefulness of "over-braining" the organisation. It emphasises the need for rationalisation in keeping with changing technological capabilities and the development of organisation structures based on modern needs.

Manpower planning is not, or should not be, some separate, rather esoteric activity carried on by a few people in back rooms in large companies. It is part of the normal conduct of business which can be and has been, successfully and advantageously practised in companies ranging widely in size, background and activity.

It will have become clear that it is a complex subject embracing the whole field of management. There is no simple tidy package; it has to be tailored to the particular business. Nevertheless, the basic principles and methods are universally applicable.

At the beginning, it can appear to be a large and somewhat daunting task; it certainly needs perseverance and determination to achieve results. It is something which is best learned by doing; and it is better to start simply, linking planning with an existing system such as annual budgeting and building from there.

## 4:12 Acknowledgement

This chapter is based on work carried out over a number of years in the British Petroleum Group. The author wishes to express his indebtedness to the many members of the staff of that company and particularly to the many staff managers of companies throughout the group for their co-operation in experimental field work and their constructive advice and criticism; to H S Mullaly, without whose support in the early, daunting stages, much less could have been accomplished; and, to former colleagues E K Ferguson and R H E Duffett, whose contribution to this work was immeasurable.

# FIVE

# Planned Training
# and Management Development

*by D S Markwell*

Planned management development has three positive aims—all designed to contribute to the efficient operation of the company. These aims are:

**1** To ensure that the company is staffed both now and in the future with sufficient managers with the necessary skills, experience and ability to secure its continued growth and profitability. This has been described as "having the right man in the right place at the right time."

**2** To check that the human resources of a company are being properly and fully used, and that potential and talent in human terms are not being overlooked or wasted but built up and allowed to grow to meet corporate needs.

**3** To provide an opportunity for staff within a company to fulfil at least some of their needs for work satisfaction and career expectations by training that will enable them to do a bigger and a richer job.

Part of the task of planned management development is to provide an appropriate fit between the expectations of the individual and the needs of the business. Management development itself derives directly from the recognition that human resources are assets like machinery, buildings and cash. As an asset, the human resource can be well used or wasted. Planned management development aims to see that human assets are properly and appropriately used (see Figure 5:1).

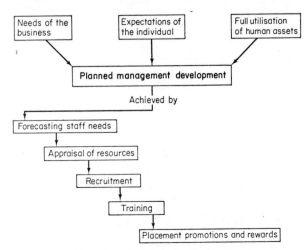

FIGURE 5:1   A MODEL FOR PLANNED
MANAGEMENT DEVELOPMENT

### 5:1 Forecasting future management requirements

Management development is not something that happens in isolation. The forecasting of management requirements in the future arises from the clear and explicit formulation of company objectives and a plan to achieve them. Company objectives likewise are translated into company plans—short, medium and long term—and the strategy by which these plans will be achieved. Plans include, and are supported by, an allocation of resources in material, cash and human terms.

It is the people that are involved that provide the starting point for a management development process. Plans may provide for new areas or methods of activity. This in turn creates a need for more and possibly different types of staff. Plans equally may provide for the discontinuance of certain types of activity. This may create a need to cope with redevelopment, redundancy and retraining. The simplest way of handling this is to draw up and compare the existing organisation chart that supports the existing operation with the organisation chart that will support the projected operations of the business derived from its forward plans. This should immediately highlight:

1    Possible redundancies
2    Recruitment needs
3    Training needs
4    Replacement needs

Thus, the charts in Figure 5:2 bring out the following points:

1    Compared with 1970, one less financial accountant's assistant is required because some work will be taken over by the computer
2    Similarly, only one customer accounts assistant and no managers will be required
3    This leaves one financial assistant and two customer accounts assistants and the customer accounts manager surplus
4    Three new posts will be created:
  (*a*)  Data processing manager
  (*b*)  Systems analyst
  (*c*)  Chief programmer
5    From experience, a wastage figure of five per cent a year is allowed

A simple comparison of charts does not give the total picture. It may identify the jobs that need to be done, but it does not itself provide enough information about the people available, their strengths, needs, potential and aspirations. This should, however, be a product of their appraisal.

Equally, the comparison of organisation charts does not provide all the facts in terms of numbers. Businesses are not static. Account must be taken of such factors as:

1    The likely wastage rate of staff over the time period from such sources as:
  (*a*)  Resignations
  (*b*)  Dismissals
  (*c*)  Unplanned retirement
       To recognise this, an appropriate wastage figure based on experience needs to be allocated intelligently to the existing resources if a projection is to be made of future needs
2    More explicitly, provision can be made for:
  (*a*)  Known retirement
  (*b*)  Planned redundancy
  (*c*)  Present vacancies

Then, having compared these two organisation charts, the business is in a position to estimate its requirements in terms of numbers, level

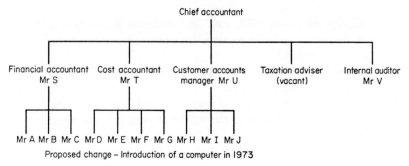

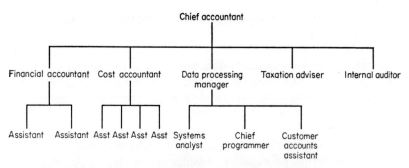

FIGURE 5:2 COMPARISON CHARTS TO INDICATE
FUTURE STAFF REQUIREMENTS
(*a*) Existing organisation chart for current operations
(*b*) Organisation chart for projected operations

and types of management it will need to fill the projected organisation chart that will support the business in, say, three years' time.

### 5:2 Appraisal of resources and identifying training needs

To satisfy future requirements an appraisal should be made of the human resources, both in terms of the jobs currently being done and in terms of potential. It is an appraisal from which real developmental needs can arise. These needs will probably be of two sorts:

1       Skill, knowledge and attitude training to perform better in
        the present job

2      Evaluation of latent ability and potential that can be built upon to produce more efficient performance now and the development of latent talent for bigger jobs in the future

The first, performance appraisal, is based on measuring actual achievement against previously agreed targets and standards of performance. It does not, however, by itself establish the basis of potential assessment.

Closely linked with performance of any sort is not just the level of knowledge, skill and experience of the individual manager but also his motivation. The degree of motivation of any manager depends in no small part on the amount of involvement and opportunity he feels he has in his job. This may also determine his training needs. The more the manager is involved with planning his work, implementing those plans and then evaluating the achievement, the more he feels committed to the activity. In addition, he becomes more able to recognise his own training needs and to establish his training plan for himself, his colleagues and his subordinates.

In performance appraisal the task of the supervisor is to check with his subordinate the level of achievement against the previously agreed work plan (see checklist in Figure 5:3). This checking process is not in itself an arbitrary operation, for not only have the manager and his subordinates previously established an agreed work plan, but they have also agreed the criteria for the judgements that will be employed in measuring success—what is sometimes called the *standard of performance* (see Figure 5:4). Obviously, these criteria cannot usefully be applied to the whole job. What they should particularly apply to is that part of the job, say 20 per cent of it, which produces say 80 per cent of the total result. Other aspects, especially those constituting special problem areas, can also be added but the focus of attention should normally be on the main tasks. These are those parts of the job without which the job cannot be said to have been performed.

The type of performance criteria that may be applied to management performance would be:

1      Quantity—tasks completed, number of items produced, and so on

2      Quality—of advice, managerial aptitude, and so on

3      Time—meeting deadlines, delivery dates or other time limits.

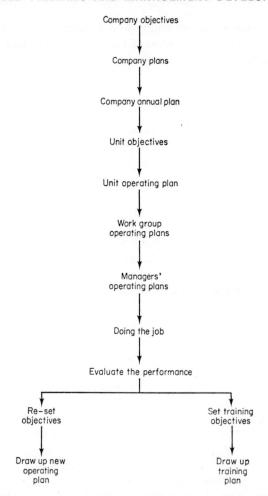

FIGURE 5:3  TRAINING IN THE WORK CONTEXT

From the performance appraisal or review—which in itself is only the formalisation of the day to day contact between the supervisor and the subordinate—many needs will arise. These are likely to be of three main types:

**1**  *Knowledge needs.* The individual may need to know more about a particular subject or skill, such as accounting, network analysis.
**2**  *Attitude needs.* The manager may be less co-operative, too defensive, less committed than he should be.

| MAIN TASK | STANDARD | CONTROL (Information required) |
|---|---|---|
| To plan and control resources at the factory | 1 To know six weeks in advance when the factory will not be able to meet a sales requirement in terms of production<br>2 Services supplied by or to the factory are agreed with the user or supplier in advance | Weekly production and raw materials supply figures<br>Personal observations<br>Comments of departmental heads<br>Dates |

FIGURE 5:4 EXTRACT FROM FACTORY
MANAGER'S WORK PLAN
Showing standards of performance

3 *Training needs.* To overcome these problems, training that will open up communication, develop trust and frankness within the work group may be required. There are three areas of relationship that are particularly important: that between individuals, that between different groups, departments or functions and that between the chief executive and his subordinate.

Ideally, the more the manager is given the opportunity to recognise his own training needs, to plan these in relation to his job and as a result recognise improvement in his work, the more likely the training activity is to be successful.

Training needs, however, do not only arise from performance in the present job. They also arise from the recognition of the man's potential for a higher job and preparing him for it. Decisions on what these training needs are to develop potential for cannot easily be made by the man himself or, indeed, even by his immediate supervisor. Decisions about the training required to equip a man to fill a higher post in the organisation is best identified by the senior management who know the demands of a job at a more senior level.

It should be recognised that senior jobs are not only quantitatively more demanding than lower level jobs but are also qualitatively different. Whereas the departmental manager is basically working within clearly specified areas of operation defined for him by the board, the general manager is working in much less closely defined areas. His job is to integrate the different departments and functions in the company and to integrate the company within its external environment, including shareholders, customers, trade unions, government, competitors, market and technological development. These are areas over which he has little, if any, control but all of which can considerably affect his operation.

For this reason the task of thinking about the potential of a man and planning the training for him to reach that potential is very much the responsibility of top management. Consultation with the man himself is important, if only because he needs to know where he is going and why the training is important.

The company must also give some attention to the man's own expectations and aspirations. Increasingly managers, as people and for their own sake, want to feel fully utilised. People resent being treated as if they are used only as an extension of the mechanics of the company. It would be inappropriate, for example, to train a young accountant to be more efficient in an accounting job, if he wants to change functions and become a sales manager or a computer specialist. In such circumstances the training the company is planning may completely miss the point and the conflict between the man's own aspirations and what the company assumes he will do may make the whole training operation less than effective.

## 5:3   Classification of training needs

In any work situation, training needs arise from three sources and these provide the springboard from which training can be undertaken. The sources are:

1   The company
2   The group
3   The individual

Many businesses are good at meeting one or other of these but rarely all three. It is in trying to strike a balance between them that the manager becomes particularly vulnerable unless he is able to see the way in which one particular set of needs integrate with all the others.

*Company needs.* The training needs that relate to the company as a whole are those that arise from the company's longer term plans and its adaptation to meet the future. They take little account of the individual but provide the company with the opportunity to move towards its goals, given the resources that are available to it. Company needs are best identified by the concern with longer term strategies and management planning. However, they will inevitably describe what should be, rather than what is or is likely to be, at least for the time being. From company needs can be designed the sort of training activities which affect the business as a whole and the managers of high potential who are to fill the more significant jobs in the future.

*Group needs.* The training needs of a work group, that is, the group manager and his subordinates, are more likely to be of immediate application and importance. They relate to the skills that the group has, either collectively or among its individual members, to fulfil the on-going job in an optimum way. Group needs are needs both to do more efficiently the job that has to be done now and also for the sort of training that enables the group to make a more significant contribution to the business and particularly to develop the latent resources that may, with training, enable the group to make a more significant contribution to the business and particularly to develop the latent resources that may, with training, enable the group to be even more effective.

Group needs cannot be readily analysed by those outside the group because it is those who have to do the job who are most likely to be aware of their shortcomings on the one hand and the under-utilisation of their resources on the other. It is an area that should be analysed by the work group itself and plans made for fulfilling their objectives by the total group. The total group can be very conscious of the way in in which it can become more efficient as a work organism, provided it is given both knowledge of the job it has to do now and in the future and is able to develop the skill to analyse its own resources frankly and openly and consider the strengths it has to make a bigger contribution in the future.

This very activity may itself throw up a considerable training need, that for the group to be able to monitor and analyse its own performance and potential in a frank and open way. To do this it will be very dependent on supportive roles within the group, each member of the group having a desire and willingness to contribute to the totality of the group's activity and to support one another in optimising the group's total performance. This implies the development and existence of a high level of trust and interdependence between members of the group. Perhaps one of the most useful training tasks that a manager of such a group can undertake is the building up of this degree of trust. It is obviously always simple for a manager to prescribe what should be done and to allocate responsibility, and then to provide rewards and blame as a result of what has been done. However, in work terms and in training terms, it is more positive if the manager can build up among his work force the openness and trust that will encourage them to ask questions about how well they are doing in their job and the way in which they could make a more efficient or greater contribution in the future. Such questions will inevitably result in training plans for the group itself.

As an example, the group may find, in reviewing its work activity, that while it is in most activities reasonably efficient, it is weak both as a group and as individuals in their planning. A result of this may be to develop a training exercise which will encourage members of the group and provide them with the skills to plan better. For example, a short on-the-job course in network planning may be helpful.

*Individual needs.* The man's needs are those arising both from his performance and from his potential. In a significant way he is well placed to identify his own needs provided he develops the skills associated with honesty and frankness about his own performance. He will not, however, have all the information to make this assessment himself, because the performance of any manager, and certainly his potential, is a product not just of his own self-analysis but of his interaction with his superior, subordinates and colleagues. It is important, therefore, in analysing his training needs, both for his present performance and for his potential, that the individual should actively seek the advice and help of those with whom his job leads him to interact. Similarly, those with whom he does interact can help him enormously in knowing more about himself and the way his performance affects others so as to help him to design his own training and development plan.

Subordinates can contribute as much as superiors to the training plan of the individual manager, particularly at the stage when they know more about the job that has to be done than he does. As an example, the new store manager may benefit as much from the training plan suggested by his new staff as from that suggested by head office and his retiring superior. In other words, in looking at the training plan, even of the individual, the help, advice and feed-back that others can give is obviously of importance. Both in developing training and in terms of the contribution that can be made by individuals to other individuals, the importance of the "helping relationship" should not be underestimated. Every person in the work situation has something to contribute and some help to give in planning training.

## 5:4 Organising the training programme

Once the training needs are recognised the training officer or management development manager can help translate them into actual operational training plans for the next work period. In this sense the training officer acts as a consultant or adviser to the individual, the work group or the company to help them achieve their training objectives. The training officer cannot, and should not, prescribe training. He can help line management analyse their problems and suggest ways in which these might be translated into training plans where a training ingredient is appropriate to help them. He is in no position either to know what the problems are or to suggest training until needs have been recognised.

Perhaps the greatest weakness of much training that has been undertaken in industry is that it has arisen from training officers prescribing training that is not necessarily related to needs, no matter how attractive or contemporary the training may appear to be. Many businesses have spent a great deal of money and time training people in skills, knowledge or techniques which have then set about seeking problems. All training should be a result of needs. These needs will be first recognised and identified by line management.

The simplest method of identifying training needs is the process of evaluation that goes on within the company at its annual review of performance, for the work groups at their monthly or bi-monthly review of their effectiveness and for the individual at his regular appraisal sessions of both his performance and potential. This process of evaluation not only feeds back into the system of the company information about development and training needs but also enables the initial setting of training plans at the various levels. As these plans in turn become part of the evaluation process, the re-setting of training plans is closely associated with all evaluation exercises. It is in helping to set and meet these plans that the training role is fulfilled.

## 5:5 Levels of training

For the individual and within the work group there are two basic levels of training to be undertaken. The first is that connected with the induction of the group or new members to it. This includes not only familiarisation with the work situation but also training of a sort which brings the work group or the individual up to the minimum standard of knowledge, skill and behaviour which enables them to fulfil their job.

There are minimum areas of knowledge and skill that the individual may bring to the job. More frequently he has to be trained before he can achieve even a basic level of performance. This "minimum performance training" is essential to the operation of any job. It can usually be undertaken in a fairly informal way as the work group develops experience and knowledge of its own tasks and is frequently based on the help that the older members of the group can and should be willing to give to newer members. However, it is an area in which considerable help can be given by a standard training pattern which might include, for example, the opportunity to observe other members of the group working, a guided reading programme and planned relevant discussions with other members of the work group or outside it.

The second level of training is that which enables the adequately performing individual or work group, both to improve its performance and perhaps even to make better use of the resources which exist within it. This is important not just for the work satisfaction that it provides for the individual but also because it ensures optimum usage of the human assets of a business. The wastage of human assets through under-utilisation is possibly one of the most besetting sins of business. This is the opportunity for the group to put all its effort behind the task to be done so that people within the group not only feel job satisfaction but, from the point of view of the business, are being fully utilised and are therefore more productive units within the company structure. For this type of training, seminars within the job context are most likely to be significant and successful. This is particularly true when they are a shared activity by all the members of a work group who see both the relevance of the seminar and its application to their particular problems.

Sometimes, however, it may be in the best interests of the group to send one of its members outside the group for training so that he can, on his return, help the others. This is most successful when the group agrees that this is what should be done, otherwise the individual being trained can easily find himself unrelated to the rest of the group on his return. If, however, the group sends him and expects him to help them on his return, he has not only a good reason for going, he has acceptance and a role to fulfil when he returns.

## 5:6 Principles of training methods

There are two main principles for those concerned with training within the business situation. These are both related to the way in which managers in a post-experience situation learn. The first is that managers learn best when they can see the relevance of what they are learning to the jobs that they have to do. This principle is a simple recognition that the manager's job is, for most of the time, a highly structured experience. He is dealing with issues and problems which come to him through his mail, his telephone or his door. He has little time to speculate and even less time to conceptualise. Even if he has time to involve himself in more theoretical speculation, that is not usually what he is employed to do. The problem solving task is an important part of his job and any training that he can recognise as relevant to his job is usually welcomed.

The second principle is what is sometimes called the *heuristic principle*. The manager learns best when he has an opportunity to try out his learning in either a real life situation or a simulated real life situation. When the manager is able to try out his learning, he is replicating the way in which he handles problems in daily life. Normally he will think through a problem to a solution, then try it out in practice and, if it works, stay with it so long as it remains appropriate. If it does not meet his needs, he will reject it and start again. When a company wishes to design training events for its management, these events are most likely to be successful, therefore, when they approximate as closely as possible to real life. Hence the training that is clearly relevant to the man's or the group's problems and which provide him with the opportunity to try out the things he learnt, is the sort of training that in most circumstances will be successful.

## 5:7 Areas of training

In thinking about the sorts of training events that can be designed, businesses have traditionally focused their attention on courses. Perhaps, worse still, not just the courses which are custom built to meet their needs but which result from a search of the open market. However, if the two principles of learning mentioned above are to be kept in mind, the company is fortunate indeed if it is able to find courses which are as relevant as they might be and which provide an opportunity to try out to the extent that they should. Furthermore, the very demands of most jobs make it extremely difficult for courses, which are time consuming, to do much more than provide some sort of support for many

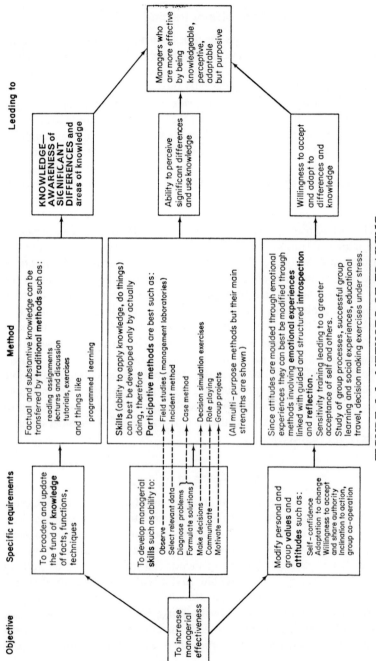

FIGURE 5:5  METHODS OF TRAINING

other types of learning activity which need to go on. At best, training given through courses supplements the total learning that a manager requires but probably never forms more than ten per cent of his total learning experience. Figure 5:5 lays out the areas of training need and the types of training appropriate.

The areas in which training can be given fall roughly into three main sub-divisions:

1     Knowledge
2     Skill
3     Attitude

Courses are to some extent appropriate to the first, to a lesser extent appropriate to the area of skill and experience and hardly appropriate at all to the area of the manager's attitude to change.

*Knowledge.* The basic knowledge that a manager requires for his job usually comes from his pre-employment or early employment education. This can frequently be provided by means of courses at universities, colleges and similar institutions. However, in the work situation, especially with post-experience managers, the usefulness of guided reading assignments should not be overlooked, particularly when coupled with a tutorial role provided by an experienced manager. This is certainly helpful during the early training of a man when he is being brought up to the required level of knowledge to fulfil his job within his department.

A second type of knowledge training is the short seminar or discussion within the work context or closely associated with it. This has the advantage not only that it provides the opportunity to draw on examples from the work environment but also because it concentrates on a specific area or topic. Experience teaches that managers rarely benefit from training activities which have a large number of learning goals. A course may, for example, include excellent contributions in the area of corporate planning, behavioural sciences, business economics and marketing but the very fact that these are confined within one total learning experience tends to diminish the amount of learning that comes in any one area. If the different subjects are dealt with independently they are more likely to be learnt effectively.

There is no work experience that does not provide learning. Unfortunately, some of the learning is not as good as it should be and some may even be potentially harmful. However, the manager needs not only the opportunity to evaluate the learning he is getting from his job activity but his learning will certainly be enhanced if he can discuss it with a wise and experienced colleague. One of the most useful aspects of on-the-job training is, therefore, for the man's superior or, if there are others more able to do it, another senior colleague, to act as his tutor with whom he can discuss the implications of what he has learnt and the value and significance of his reviewing his observations and his experience. Too little use is commonly made of this tutorial role of the senior colleague.

There are certain types of knowledge, particularly of techniques, which can be efficiently taught by such methods as programmed learning. The advantage of this type of approach is that it provides the manager with a monitor of his own progress. He is able to check himself and his learning in a significant way. Where this system is appropriate, it is often possible for the manager to undertake a considerable amount of training for himself.

All the above types of training happen basically within the context of the job. Managers with the responsibility for training their staff and themselves should see that time is available to undertake this learning and that progress with it, life job progress, is systematically reviewed.

*Skills and experience.* The development of skill in using techniques and the growth of management experience is obviously much more related to doing the job than it is to any sort of formal learning and it is in this area that career planning and the proper deployment of people become particularly important. There should be some clear view taken by the top management of the company, and particularly for those people of higher potential, about the sort of jobs and the sorts of work environment in which they should be working to prepare themselves for the future.

It is rarely possible in a work situation to be over-specific, certainly over a long period, about particular jobs that a man might do. It should, however, be possible to specify the sort of jobs that he should be involved in. Let us assume that a man is considered, as a result of performance and potential appraisals, to be a future managing director of a subsidiary unit. If he has a predominantly accounting background, it is important that before he moves to the managing director's job he should have some experience which gives him an understanding of the marketing, distribution and sales aspects of a company's operation, the personnel aspects of its working and the technical and production responsibility. In addition, if it is at all possible for him to have experience of working as a personal assistant to an experienced managing director before he takes up his own responsibility, his preparation for the new job will be considerably increased.

The rate of change in the areas of management today often prevents the company from providing the man with all the experience that may be desirable. To overcome this disadvantage, certain types of learning events can, at least in part, replace actual experience. Such events would include things like special investigation assignments and the careful study, analysis and evaluation of case material, particularly if drawn from real life and in which the manager himself is able to consult with those who were involved. Decision making exercises and management games provide another sort of simulated experience. Role playing and group projects, in which he is involved in discussions with others and brought to the position where he must reach consensus, can supplement his planned work experience and provide him with opportunity and experience in developing the knowledge that he has.

*Attitude.* Unlike knowledge, attitudes are a result rather more of conditioning and emotional experiences than they are of what the manager knows. To develop or modify attitudes and behaviour, learning events that are more orientated to feelings than to knowledge become important. The manager may know that he should co-operate with his colleagues. He may have attended many courses on good human relations; but until he experiences and feels the advantages of co-operation with others, his knowledge will have little application.

The areas of attitude with which a company is particularly concerned are such as building up a manager's self-confidence, his adaptation to change, and his willingness to accept and share authority and to co-operate with others in the achievement of objectives. Some of this type of experience undoubtedly comes from the work situation in which he finds himself. However, it is important that he reflects in a systematic and conscious way upon what he has learned from co-operation.

In this area of attitude development it is also possible to shorten the process of learning from the job itself by using the techniques and methods of organisational development training. Basically, these methods teach a work group to monitor its own performance, identify its own problems and reach consensus in an open and frank way. Reviewing and working together as a group for a short period can help this process. Similarly, certain types of business exercises and games operated under stress conditions can complement this attitude-development training.

The purpose of all methods of training is not to be an end in themselves but to improve the effectiveness both of the individual and of the company in the job that has to be done. Within the business context, even under conditions in which industrial training boards operate, the objective of training is to enhance the effectiveness of the company, the group and the individual.

## 5:8   The place of courses in training

In many instances a course has more than one objective, not just in terms of knowledge but in terms of experience, development and attitude change. The type of course that is employed is that which is geared to the particular needs of the individual or the group. It is impossible in most work situations to custom-build every learning experience for every particular individual or situation. Some evaluation criteria is therefore desirable to make the optimum use of courses. In evaluating whether or not a course is appropriate to meet a particular need, the criteria mentioned in the following paragraphs may act as a guide.

*Conceptualisation.* It is important to ask how far the course provides the opportunity for the manager to look not just at a particular piece of knowledge or technique, but to understand the issues that it raises. For example, a course on productivity bargaining which deals only with the techniques of bargaining and not with the issues in a bargaining situation and the feelings, attitudes and concepts of the parties involved, would be less useful than one which raised the issues as well as the methods.

*Business goals.* Not all businesses have identified goals except in very general terms. A course appropriate for the business that has short term, high profit goals may be quite inappropriate for the business that has longer term interests. It should be possible to reconcile the sort of business philosophy that the course is advocating with the philosophy and culture of the company in which the man to be trained is working.

*Research.* In an age of proliferation of management training activities, many top managers are becoming increasingly suspicious of the "new" or "contemporary" approach. A course, and any new concepts it introduces, must be clearly based on research studies which are validated and significant—not on the feeling and opinions of a good salesman for his particular breed of management education. This does not necessarily mean that research-based training must employ research of only an academically rigorous kind. Indeed, research based on things which have actually happened in companies, as distinct from laboratory situations, can be more useful and valuable to the manager being trained.

*Participation.* In his ordinary life at work, the manager learns by means of interaction with his colleagues. The post-experience manager no longer accepts the teacher/student relationship which he may willingly have accepted in his undergraduate days. Furthermore, he has himself a great deal of opinion, experience and a point of view to contribute to most management learning situations. He will welcome in a course the opportunity to share his views and experience with those of the contributors who are running the course, because this is similar to the way in which he learns on the job at work and the way he expects to be treated as an individual.

*Environment.* The course is likely to be helpful to the manager when the environment is one in which he is able to display unembarrassed ignorance. If, because he is going to be reported on or because he does not want to display a lack of knowledge in front of superiors, colleagues and friends, he is inhibited from expressing an opinion or asking questions, his learning will not be as great as it will be if he feels he has greater freedom. An environment in which he can be totally open and in which he is encouraged to display his ignorance will provide him with a better learning opportunity than one which restricts him.

*Level.* Many courses fail to recognise the difference in level that exists within a business and accept too wide a range of membership. Not only does this wide range have certain limiting sociological characteristics, but, more importantly, it does not give the manager the feeling that the learning is relevant to his job. Many courses invite the young trainee to pretend that he is on the board of a company, an experience which, fascinating though it may be to him, is a long way removed from the realities of the job that he is likely to be doing, not only in the immediate future but also in the foreseeable future. Unless the level is right for the man, it could create frustration and feelings of dissatisfaction which, rather than helping him in his work, may hinder him.

*Qualifications.* The qualifications, both academic and practical, of those who presume to direct courses and teach on them are important, not only for their own sake but also in terms of the degree of credibility that, as contributors, they will have to the operating line manager. The consultant or the academic teacher is unlikely to be as acceptable as a teacher as a man who can draw on a knowledge and experience of business.

*Change.* In evaluating the courses that are available for management training, thought needs to be given to their growth. Management itself in the 1970s is highly dynamic. Courses that do not respond to these changes are rarely as useful as those which are consciously keeping abreast of, or a little ahead of, the work environment.

*Monitoring.* The course should provide the manager with the opportunity to check what he has learnt against the background to which he will be returning. There is no more disillusioning experience for a manager on a course than to find that the things which sounded credible in the context of a course experience become irrelevant when related to the facts of real life. The course should provide an opportunity to check experience and understand, preferably in conjunction with more experienced line managers, the concepts and ideas that have been developed on the course. Only in this way is the manager in a position to transfer his learning back to the job situation.

### 5:9 Preparing the training guide

Although thought has been given to the way in which training needs can be established and training plans developed, it is obviously a waste of time and energy to repeat this on every single occasion. It is possible, however, to develop a training guide which can provide the basic checklist for any given job. This will help not only to identify the particular training needs of the individual or the group but also to suggest possible methods by which these needs might be met.

Recognising that the needs of the individual or the group vary according to the personalities, education and experience of the people involved, there are, nevertheless, some common areas applicable to a wide range of people within a particular function and at similar levels within an organisation. Further, there are some aspects which are common to many functions within an organisation. These can be built into a training guide.

Any training guide needs development in particular circumstances to meet the further needs of an individual but the very existence of a checklist provides a basis on which training can be developed. The existence of the guide may give an indication of areas within which training should be developed in the future and at different stages in the development of the individual.

In implementing a training plan, however, the full range of training methods need to be employed, some of which have already been discussed. More importantly, unless there is a clear view of the training need and a suitable method of training is found, it is likely that excessive use will be made of the course activity. Courses should be seen only as support to and extension of training received on the job. The remainder of this chapter is a schedule that has been developed as a training guide for buyers. It is not exclusive and, of course, covers many other aspects of training than those specifically designed for the buying function. In the schedule, courses have been used only where other methods of training cannot be used instead and, as such, it may provide an example of the type of check list which can be developed in any given situation. As experience develops, training guides of this type for buyers can be developed for other major functions within an organisation and, as such, provide a systematic and on-going reminder of areas of training which the manager, in considering both his own needs and those of his subordinates for development, could or should be working.

## TRAINING NEEDS FOR BUYERS
BASIC KNOWLEDGE AND SKILLS

## SUGGESTED METHODS OF ACHIEVEMENT

1 Knowledge of suppliers, their products, organisation and financial structure

Visits, reports, use of trade literature—collection and extraction. Specialist seminars provided by manufacturers and associations

2 Information concerning commodity, product or service, including processes and product cost analysis

3 Knowledge of specific supply markets and their mechanisms

4 Understanding of political, economic, social and climatic influences on supplies and markets

Product surveys. Press reports. E & S surveys. Visits to or contacts with commodity exchanges and information agencies (E & S, embassies, marketing boards, overseas trade agencies)

5 An awareness of the opportunities and hazards in supply markets and of how to react to them

Discussion sessions with departmental manager. Buying courses

| | | |
|---|---|---|
| 6 | An understanding of the nature and value of considerations other than price: ability to weigh these against each other | Guided experience. Buying courses |
| 7 | Understanding of contract terms (financial, insurance, transport and shipping), what they imply and how they can best be used | Guided reading. Visits to specialist departments. Buying courses |
| 8 | Understanding of capital and financial criteria (investment decisions, cash flow and payback, cost of capital and risk of various sorts) | Guided reading. Discussion. Accounts courses |
| 9 | Knowledge of the company he is buying for, its objectives and products, its marketing and manufacturing methods, so as to appreciate the possibilities and constraints of any situation | Induction programme. Visits to departments |
| 10 | Stock control systems and associated mathematical techniques | Guided reading. Programmed learning. Various courses |
| 11 | Negotiating skills | Experience, especially from accompanying seniors. Buying courses |

ASSOCIATED KNOWLEDGE AND SKILLS

| | | |
|---|---|---|
| 1 | Linguistic ability—English and appropriate other languages | Language laboratory. Records and tapes |
| 2 | Good command of the use of native language, both spoken and written | Guidance on the job. Report writing. Report writing courses. Public speaking course |
| 3 | Ability to chair and contribute to a meeting | Guided experience, such as sitting in on meetings. Practical seminars |
| 4 | Ability to explore and analyse figures | Programmed learning. Quantitative concepts courses |
| 5 | Appreciation of the commercial uses of computers | On the job applications. Computer courses |
| 6 | Relevant knowledge of economics, including the build-up of accounting costs and the difference between accounting costs and economic costs | Guided reading |
| 7 | Understanding of legal obligations and the law as it affects buyers, sellers and users of goods and services, patents | Guided reading. Talks. Various courses |

| | | |
|---|---|---|
| 8 | Knowledge of areas or arrangements in which deals could be illegal, such as purchase of firearms, purchase tax, drugs, currency and exchange deals, customs duty evasion | Guided reading. Talks |
| 9 | Appreciation of company standards of ethics and fair dealing | Induction. Guidance and example |
| 10 | Understanding of the importance of security and the ways in which it can be protected | Induction. Guidance and example |
| 11 | Recognition of hazards to property and safety of people | Induction. Guidance and example |
| 12 | Optimisation techniques, such as value analysis, linear programming | On the job applications. Various courses |
| 13 | The use and costs of alternative communications media | Induction and guidance |

MANAGERIAL/ORGANIZATIONAL
KNOWLEDGE AND SKILLS

| | | |
|---|---|---|
| 1 | An understanding of his company's organisation and channels for communication | Induction and updating |
| 2 | A knowledge and understanding of the planning processes of his company | Induction and guided experience. Temporary attachment to planning section |
| 3 | A knowledge of the activities of other company's buying departments operating in his field | Visits |
| 4 | Knowledge of other departmental functions affecting his job— quality control, transport, production, engineering, advertising, development, cost and financial accounting, planning | Induction. Visits. Discussions with other specialists |
| 5 | A thorough knowledge and understanding of the policies and procedures within his own department | Induction and guidance. Operating documents |
| 6 | To know and understand all company policies and procedures impinging on buying | Operating documents and counselling by departmental manager |
| 7 | Knowledge of (a) company policies in relation to recruitment, training, appraisal, development, promotion and placement | Operating documents and counselling by departmental manager. Buying courses |

(*b*) training methods and means of self-development

| | | |
|---|---|---|
| 8 | Knowledge of his responsibilities and of the extent of his authority | Job description and counselling by departmental manager |
| 9 | Ability to organise his work, to set targets, to operate within a plan, to contribute to company plans and to select priorities | Guided experience and target setting |
| 10 | Job analysis and methods study | Guided experience. Various courses |

PERSONAL QUALITIES AND BEHAVIOURAL AWARENESS

| | | |
|---|---|---|
| 1 | Ability to manage staff and to maximise individual and group effort | |
| 2 | Ability to gain acceptance, respect and trust from colleagues and suppliers | Guided experience. Reading. Seminars (communications, group relations and so on) |
| 3 | Ability to communicate effectively and maintain good personal relations at all levels and in all circumstances | |
| 4 | Commercial judgement and discretion | Guided experience. Case studies |
| 5 | Skills of observation. The ability to listen. The specific skill of "being informed". | |
| 6 | Ability to recognise information which is useful and worth collecting; recognition of inconsistencies which need further investigation | Special projects. Guided experience |
| 7 | Ability to work and make positive decisions under pressure | Guided experience. Case studies |
| 8 | Generation of new ideas and policies, and ability to secure implementation | Guided experience. Special projects |

# SIX

# Planning Mergers and Acquisitions

*by N A M Eastwood*

The basic rules for success in merging include the setting of objective and realistic requirements, good planning and good decision-making, a determination to take people into account, and a degree of generosity when it comes to sharing out the benefits.

In speaking of mergers one tends to include the acquisition of a small company by a larger company as well as the true merger of two companies of comparable size. The terminology is not important, though the word 'takeover' has become an emotive word and is best avoided. There are many so-called types of mergers—horizontal, vertical, diversification, financial, conglomerate—and there are also negative mergers—divestments and "spin offs." Before discussing the modern approach to mergers it is of interest to look at the development of mergers historically, and perhaps try to extrapolate current trends into the future.

### 6:1  Merger patterns in recent years

Mergers really became news following the Second World War. There had always been mergers and acquisitions, generally among the smaller companies, though it was in the inter-war years that many of the great industrial groupings were formed. The difficult years of the early thirties created the environment which made it attractive for companies to group together for strength. Many of the companies merging in this period were finding progress difficult; some were probably insolvent.

Within groups they did not always survive in a recognisable form but the aim was often solely to preserve their skills and their market positions.

The mergers which followed the 1939–45 war were different. During the war controls on profit making, at a time when many companies were more profitable than ever before, produced a state of affairs in which companies were under-valued while being unusually strong in terms of assets. Wartime profits had been held down, while peacetime profits in the austerity era were depressed for other reasons, resulting in unexciting valuations based on profits. At the same time companies were rich in assets, for a number of reasons. Wartime earnings had been channelled back into re-equipment and stockbuilding, where this was possible. In addition, many companies gained from the "free issue" of plant and equipment paid for by the government for munitions production, which was later taken into companies' books at low values. After the war property began to boom, but properties in most companies' books remained at pre-war values.

The mergers of the fifties were based mainly on the exploitation of these situations. Swollen asset companies were acquired at well below their real values—and it was not unusual for the price to be half the true valued assets acquired. These were essentially financial mergers, but in many cases this served as a base on which large industrial and commercial groupings could be logically constructed.

In the sixties financial situations were becoming harder to find and the overall basis for merging moved towards industrial and commercial reorganisation—a phrase covering a multitude of motives!

According to government statistics covering acquisitions by public companies, the number of acquisitions made in a year has risen considerably over the years, though the pace is now steadier. The majority of acquisitions are those of private companies by public companies, where the increase has been pronounced. The average size of acquired public companies, in terms of price paid for them, continues to increase. This does not apply to the private companies, where size of acquisition appears steadier.

The figures shown in Table 6:1 cover all sizes of companies; more detailed statistics are available covering the larger companies and these show an interesting switch. In the late fifties companies tended to join with other companies within their own industrial classifications. The overall industry figure in 1958–60 was 62 per cent merging within the same classification —manufacturing alone was higher at 66 per cent, while for distribution and services the figure was only 44 per cent. By 1966–8 the overall figure

| | PUBLIC COMPANIES | | PRIVATE COMPANIES | | TOTAL MERGERS |
|---|---|---|---|---|---|
| | No. | Average price £m | No. | Average price £m | No. |
| 1954 | 42 | | 233 | | 275 |
| 1955 | 49 | | 245 | | 294 |
| 1956 | 44 | | 202 | | 246 |
| 1957 | 70 | | 231 | | 301 |
| 1958 | 60 | | 280 | | 340 |
| 1959 | 98 | | 461 | | 559 |
| 1960 | 81 | | 655 | | 736 |
| 1961 | 64 | | 568 | | 632 |
| 1962 | 62 | 3.1 | 574 | 0.29 | 636 |
| 1963 | 77 | 2.3 | 808 | 0.22 | 885 |
| 1964 | 71 | 3.7 | 868 | 0.39 | 939 |
| 1965 | 75 | 4.7 | 920 | 0.18 | 995 |
| 1966 | 78 | 4.3 | 727 | 0.17 | 805 |
| 1967 | 97 | 6.8 | 666 | 0.29 | 763 |
| 1968 | 154 | 9.3 | 788 | 0.41 | 942 |

(Comparable figures for 1969 and 1970 not available.)

TABLE 6:1  ACQUISITIONS IN GREAT BRITAIN BY
QUOTED COMPANIES FROM 1954–68

for the same classification mergers was down to 48 per cent, with distribution and service down to 28 per cent and manufacturing at 53 per cent. Clearly the trend is towards more interesting, though not necessarily more constructive mergers.

Over the same period the average size of mergers—based on net assets transferred—quadrupled overall, with the greater growth being in manufacturing. Even allowing for the changing value of money, the average size doubled.

Although the figures may suggest a slowing trend, this may be temporary. The difficulties which currently face industry and commerce are now really beginning to bite. The solution to many companies' problems will lie in a suitable merger. The entry of the UK into the EEC will mean greater competition and greater opportunities for many companies: meeting competition with strength and exploiting opportunities with appropriate skills will demand many mergers. One can therefore envisage a growth in merger activity, and in time this will include a more significant proportion of mergers with continental companies.

## 6:2  Strategic factors—offensive and defensive

Some companies' objectives may only be attainable through a suitable merger; in many other cases an important factor is that objectives can be attained earlier through a merger than by the process of internal development and growth.

A company's strategic aims will be either offensive or defensive. The prime offensive aim will be the location of new growth areas of business, coupled with the early exploitation of such areas. This presupposes that a company growing at an above average rate continually requires new fields to exploit; in general this is a fair supposition. There is also the tactical factor that a merger may make it possible for a company to exploit existing fields more profitably.

There are three important defensive factors. The foremost factor stems from the recognition that a field currently being exploited has begun to decline in profitability or size and that a switch of resources to a new field is desirable, probably by way of a merger. The diversification of the tobacco giants is a good example.

Also defensive is the requirement for a company to protect its lines of supply, so that its own trading ability will not be compromised by the failure or takeover of an important supplier by a competitor.

But of major strategic significance is the defensive need to avoid being taken over by an undesirable party. Here, size alone plays an important part, while the financial engineering that can be achieved through a merger can also add a degree of complexity which may thwart an unwanted bidder.

There are other factors worth mentioning. Small companies may equally well feel the need to be acquired. The main offensive reason is usually that they have opportunities or skills to exploit, but they lack the resources with which to do so. They can justly seek to sell to a bigger company at a good price. In the defensive context the small company may feel weak, may see its current trading diminishing, or may fear an unwanted takeover. A sale to an appreciative larger company may well be the solution, though the price may not be so attractive.

There are also personal reasons for selling a small company. Successful proprietors who have built a business often wish to sell out in order to enjoy the results of their labours. For others, not so keen to sell out, they do so because of the difficulties of working with close-company and other recent legislation. Finally, there is always the need for proprietors to provide against death duty.

There are also personal factors at play among the acquirors, and these can be dangerous. Mergers are sometimes arranged for the comfort of directors, without there being other and more constructive benefits, and often to the detriment of shareholders. Worse are the mergers which at the best are empire-building and at the worst are exercises in the gathering of great personal power.

## 6:3   Auditing the company's present position

Planning should commence with a position audit, which in effect defines the base on which the future of the company will be built. The position audit should be an assessment of all the company's resources—these will include products, market strengths, marketing and selling organisations, research and development organisation, production (split perhaps into premises, plant and machinery, manpower, special skills), management and management development and, not least, financial resources. Each of these elements needs to be carefully assessed, both objectively and subjectively. The studies must pose the questions—where do we stand now?—what are our strengths and weaknesses?—what potential is there for the future, and what opportunities?

Finally the position audit must sum up the potential and opportunities for the whole company. This will be a long and detailed task, best done by well supervised managers than by directors. It is then the directors' task to take the position audit and ask—where do we go from here?—what should be the long term objectives of the company? This is essentially the board's most important job. The company's long term objectives must be established, not necessarily in great detail but clearly as overall aims. The board will take a bold look into the future—it will consider the possibly changing pattern of its markets and it will give thought to product development in line with this changing pattern.

The long term corporate plan follows. This will be a fairly detailed plan which will set out how the company is to achieve its objectives. The corporate plan will itself be comprised of a number of divisional plans, each in turn a composition of sub-division plans. There will be the marketing plan covering markets, products and sales, the production plan covering premises, plant and equipment and manpower and skills, the financial plan including the profit plan, cash-flow timing and working capital and fixed capital requirements, and finally the management plan covering management requirements, management development and recruitment, and systems, the most important of which will be the planning system.

From the corporate plan will come the requirement, if any, for a merger or an acquisition. The requirement may well be an essential element in the plan, or it may be featured in terms of saving time and expense.

## 6:4   Evaluating the benefits

Perhaps the most obvious benefit is that of economies of scale—two can operate proportionally more cheaply than one, though not necessarily more easily.

The reduction of competition is an important benefit, though the elimination of a competitor for no constructive reason is frowned upon. More important is the broadening of a company's competitive front by a merger or acquisition. This is especially so in the case of exporting, where it may be essential to offer a full range of products or services. Here also the competitive strength coming from a merger is important in that it can open up to a company larger and more competitive markets. This broadening of the competitive front may well be geographical, and this applies equally well at home as overseas.

An enlarged and more comprehensive product range may feature as a benefit and, whether or not allied with the broadened competitive front, this can clearly be an asset.

The acquisition of needed product and technological know-how may feature, also the acquisition of needed expertise and special skills, while the acquisition of additional good management is an important benefit often played down for obvious reasons. Then there is the reverse, where a merger or acquisition opens up new opportunities for the exercise of a company's existing special skills, and new opportunities for existing management.

Scale alone can be important, especially in manufacturing and in the ability to finance highly technical and expensive development projects. The more efficient use of selected premises and equipment may release other premises and equipment for either disposal or for use in connection with some new project, so avoiding new capital expenditure. Manpower can be more efficiently used, both in terms of supervisory and support management as well as direct labour on the job, while rate of production itself is known to produce manpower savings in many fields.

## 6:5  Financial benefits and the arithmetic of the p/e ratio

The board's objective is the most efficient use of the company's resources—primarily on behalf of shareholders, but also on behalf of employees. The yardstick here is the return on investors' capital—measured in terms of earnings per share and coupled with the growth of these earnings.

The most accepted measure of performance is currently the p/e ratio—the ratio of overall price of a share on the stock market to the net earnings for that share generated by the company. Equity earnings are the return on investors' capital: the p/e ratio used to value these earnings reflect the quality of these earnings in terms of several factors, the most important of which are the reliability of the earnings and the prospects for earnings growth.

The p/e ratio is particularly relevant to mergers. A company with a high p/e ratio can acquire another company relatively cheaply, or more economically, if the other company has a lower p/e ratio. This is best seen by reference to an example. Suppose that Company *A* makes profits after tax of £100 000, and that it can be acquired for £900 000, ie a p/e of 9. Suppose Company *B* is on a p/e ratio of say 12, and that it duly acquires *A* for an exchange of shares for £900 000. *B* gets additional post tax profits of £100 000 and, because *B* is on a p/e ratio of 12, *B*'s overall value is increased by £1 200 000 for an outlay of only £900 000. This really results from *A*'s profits becoming more highly regarded once *A* comes under control of *B*, though clearly there could be an effect on *B*'s rating if the acquisition of *A* appeared illconceived. However, it was on this piece of arithmetic that the growth of the conglomerate type of company was founded.

The high p/e arithmetic also works where money has to be raised through an equity issue in order to make an acquisition for cash.

The immediate increase in earnings per share which can be achieved through a merger can stem from either the use of a favourable p/e ratio, as already discussed, or through the addition of debt capital which will increase the company's capital gearing, or from both. Earnings per share is such an important measure as to warrant examples of how this increase happens.

Company *A* has a share capital of 1 000 000 shares and has net earnings of £200 000, or 20p per share. The shares stand at £3 per share, giving a total valuation of £3 000 000, at which the p/e ratio is therefore 15.

Company *B* has net earnings of £120 000, and *A* is able to acquire *B* for a price of £1 440 000, ie on a p/e ratio of 12. *A* acquires *B* for an exchange of shares, issuing 480 000 of its own shares, value £3 per share, total £1 440 000; or *A* acquires *B* in exchange for an issue of some form of loan stock totalling £1 440 000 in value and carrying an interest rate of say 11% (effective cost 6.6% after corporation tax.)

The effect on *A*'s earnings per share is as follows:

| COMPANY *A* | BEFORE | AFTER ACQUISITION OF *B* | |
| --- | --- | --- | --- |
| | | FOR SHARES | FOR LOAN STOCK |
| Net earnings | £200 000 | £320 000 | £320 000 |
| Less net interest charges | — | — | 95 000 |
| | £200 000 | £320 000 | £225 000 |
| Total number of shares in issue | 1 000 000 | 1 480 000 | 1 000 000 |
| Earnings per share | 20p | 21.6p | 22.5p |

There are other financial benefits. Liquidity can be improved if the acquired company has good liquidity—it may even have cash to spare, and this is one way of raising money in exchange for an issue of shares or loan stock. A merger can also improve a company's financial balance —if *A* has large profits but relatively few assets, and merges with *B* which has few profits but large assets, perhaps under-utilised, the merged entity will have better financial balance than either party by itself.

An increase in financial size, possibly with an increase in financial balance, reduces vulnerability to undesirable takeover approaches. The size of a company which can be reasonably acquired by another can vary with individual circumstances, but nevertheless there are limits. Size alone is a factor in terms of reducing vulnerability.

## 6:6 Benefits from time saved

Not only is time money, but it can mean opportunities lost if they are not seized when they occur. The development of new products and new markets do not necessarily depend on making an acquisition, but often the way to save time and money is to acquire the benefit of another company's spadework or experience.

The importance of saving time through an acquisition cannot be overestimated. The far-sighted businessman will be planning ahead for growth and looking for new opportunities. He will find the speed of change increasing and he must be ready for it and must foresee the need to change. He will need to act swiftly to seize opportunities, and suitable acquisitions will enable him to react quickly and flexibly in a changing environment.

## 6:7  Valuing a company

The method of valuation will depend on whether the company to be acquired is a public or a private company, or possibly a privately-controlled public company.

With a public company a guide to its value is clearly its stock market capitalisation. Generally shareholders can be counted upon to sell at a premium of between 20% and 50% over this market value, depending on circumstances. Examples of premiums over 50% are not too rare. However, although the market's valuation seeks to take into account all relevant factors, it may not do so as rationally as might be wished, and it is necessarily a consensus view.

Where a share has a generally dull record and uninteresting prospects, with perhaps a slack market, shareholders may be only too pleased to sell out at a small premium. But where the share is exciting, in a strong market, shareholders will hope for a counter offer and possibly an auction. It is amazing how one bid for a company is often followed by bids from other parties suddenly interested (or panicked?) into participating. In these circumstances a 50 per cent premium is not uncommon, while even 100 per cent has been seen.

Ultimately the potential acquiror must decide its maximum offer taking into account not just the earnings and the assets to be acquired, but also all the benefits which could be expected to follow from the acquisition.

How much can be paid, and the price that will be accepted are both subject to the form the purchase consideration will take. There are no firm rules; circumstances will govern the relative attractiveness of giving and accepting equity shares, loan stock, perhaps convertible, debenture, or cash.

If the acquisition is a privately-controlled public company arrangements will be necessary to win the specific support of the controlling faction, who may or may not have the same outlook as the public shareholders. This may well present personality problems.

The valuation of a private company is clearly a matter of bargaining, on the understanding that the proprietors are willing to sell at some price. Public companies are generally acquired for prices in the range of 10 to 20 times post tax earnings—p/e ratio 10 to 20. Private companies are generally acquired on p/e's of 5 to 12. But to complicate matters, negotiations usually revolve around pretax profits, which means prices of 3 to 7 times pretax profits.

While profits of public companies are fairly readily established from published accounts, the stated profits of private companies often require considerable adjustment in order to establish representative profits. A proprietor effectively taking his dividends in the form of additional director's remuneration obviously affects the profit picture.

Again it is a matter for the acquiror to decide just what it is worth paying, as a maximum. Satisfying the proprietor's personal requirements will seldom be a matter of purchase price alone. Managing proprietors will clearly be interested in their roles in the merged operation—or in the provisions to be made for retirement. Relatives too may have to be considered, also employees. In valuing a private company it is the total value of the package which counts.

Where a private company is not in a position to be valued on its profits, for various reasons, the valuation will be on the basis of its net asset value. In the absence of a profits based valuation, the price to be paid by an acquiror will seldom be more than net asset value, and will often be less; the particular circumstances will be important in relating price to the net asset value.

### 6:8   Deciding the form of the purchase consideration

There is an apparently wide choice in the form which the purchase consideration may take, but in practice circumstances ultimately dictate a fairly narrow choice, if any at all. The consideration may consist entirely of, or any combination of, equity shares; preference shares, convertible or not; loan stock, secured or unsecured, and convertible or not; or cash.

Cash is the simplest form of consideration, and often the most acceptable. But where the vendors wish to retain an interest in the future development of their company, equity shares in the merged company will be relevant.

However, from the acquiror's point of view, equity shares are an expensive form of consideration as their cost effectively mounts as the company grows and dividends are increased. Also, dividends paid on equity shares cannot be offset against profits for corporation tax purposes, as can interest on a loan stock.

Where cash is not available, loan stock may be used, but this is not so attractive to vendors, even if issued as a debenture. More attractive is convertible loan stock, giving the vendors the option to convert into equity later, but giving a better return in the meantime, and attractive to the acquiror in that the conversion price can be set at a value higher than the current equity price.

If cash is demanded by the vendors, the acquiror may be able to "place" equity or loan stock with third parties in return for cash with which to satisfy the vendors. Finally, there is the point that a cash consideration is a realisation for capital gains tax purposes, whereas a "paper" consideration is not.

## 6:9 Executing the formalities of a deal

The acquisition of a private company by another private company requires few public formalities; the same would apply to a private company acquisition by a public company of such a size that the acquisition is for cash and is not "material" within the meaning of the Stock Exchange rules for reporting material acquisitions. On the completion in principle of negotiation for $A$ to acquire $B$, $A$ would ask reporting accountants to report on the affairs of $B$, essentially in financial terms, and would ask solicitors to prepare a sale and purchase contract enjoining $A$ with the shareholders of $B$. In parallel $A$ would be making arrangements for the purchase consideration with its bankers or merchant bankers. If $A$ is a public company and is planning to issue shares or a loan stock to be quoted on a stock exchange, there will be formalities to be attended to, though these will generally be simple. The acquisition would be formally effected by the completion of the sale and purchase contract.

Where $A$ is a public company and $B$ represents a material acquisition, $A$ will have to circulate its own shareholders with full details of the acquisition, though only after the event and for information only.

Where $A$ and $B$ are both public companies, $A$ must make a formal public offer to the shareholders of $B$ to acquire their shares in $B$. This Offer is usually made by a merchant bank on behalf of $A$, and comprises a highly detailed and sophisticated document. If the Offer has the support of $B$'s board, the document will say so and will most likely include a letter of recommendation from the chairman of $B$, alongside the letter of invitation from the chairman of $A$. Where the Offer is made for $A$ by its merchant bankers there will also be reference to the merchant bank's judgment that the terms are fair and equitable to $B$'s shareholders.

The merchant bank will also set out how the purchase consideration is to be comprised, and will show its value.

Apart from partial offers, all offers will be conditional on over 50% acceptance by $B$'s shareholders, and often on 90 per cent acceptance, after which $A$ can automatically acquire the balance to 100 per cent.

The formalities with such a public offer are naturally involved, but they present few problems to the professional expertise of a merchant bank specialising in corporate finance.

If $A$'s offer is contested either by $B$'s board or by a third party making another offer, $A$ and its merchant bank may have to further demonstrate the merits of their own offer, and if necessary improve it. This will be done through further circulars and possibly a revised offer to $B$'s shareholders. Ultimately $A$ or the other bidder may decide to withdraw, or the shareholders themselves may decide by accepting one offer. The important point in such situations is that $A$ should avoid being tempted into paying more than $B$ is worth.

### 6:10   Using the services of the City

Mergers begin with corporate planning. Many of the larger public companies have developed highly sophisticated corporate planning operations. Smaller public companies rely more on outside advisers, but many are now setting up their own planning functions, perhaps two or three men under the direct control of the managing director or the planning director. In private companies the corporate planner is usually the managing director or the marketing director in person.

Corporate planning advice is available from most of the better firms of management consultants, but of recent years the more enlightened City merchant banks have begun to advise on this subject through their corporate finance departments. Their view is that the hit-and-miss approach to mergers is not good enough, and that sound planning is essential. The merchant bank or the management consultant can undertake the whole task for a company, if necessary, or, better, it can help set up a planning function within a company using the company's own people and can then help guide the team. For all but the largest companies with their own teams, some degree of outside advice and consultation is desirable, if not essential.

The search for the right acquisition should also be a joint effort. The seeking company will have defined what it is looking for with the help of its advisers. In addition to help in the search from merchant banks with their own very extensive intelligence and information networks, there are the services of the specialist merger brokers.

When a suitable acquisition has been identified an approach must be made, with appropriate delicacy, and negotiations commenced. At this stage a merchant bank is essential if the deal is to be other than of minimal size, when the services of the company's solicitors or accountants may suffice.

The services of solicitors and accountants will in any case be necessary beyond this stage, and it should be remembered that they can help in many ways at earlier stages. The firms used should be those accustomed to this type of work—indeed the retention of professionals inexperienced in this particular field can be dangerous.

The merchant bank will be responsible for carrying through the negotiations, including advising and negotiating on the price, and will advise on raising the purchase consideration. Finally, the merchant bank will take care of the formalities.

The overall conduct of all parties, principals and advisers, is subject to the Takeover Code; adherence to the Code is firmly supervised by the Takeover Panel. The Code itself is a sensible and generally easily worked code of practice governing all parties. Its main aim, which no fair-minded person need fear, is to protect the interests of all parties, including shareholders, from both apparent and actual unfair practice that might otherwise be suggested in a takeover situation, whether contested or not.

### 6:11 Managing the intangible aspects of a merger

Success in merging is to do with people. Failure of a commercial enterprise to operate successfully can probably be attributed more to people failures than to any other cause. And this doesn't just mean "other" people—it means one's own team and one's own self.

Apart from people, there is scope for ultimate failure at almost every stage before and after the actual merger event. The approach to a merger, the strategic planning, the search and investigation phase, the negotiations and the acquisition itself and how these are all carried out are just as important in achieving success as the moves which take place after the deal is done.

The failure to clarify motives is a prime source of overall failure. Acquirors must clearly establish just what they want to achieve by an acquisition. Then, having decided what they should look for, very serious consideration must be given to establishing whether any given acquisition will, or will not, allow this to be achieved. Consideration must be given to whether the deal itself, or in its effect on people and on commercial ties, will compromise any of the desired benefits.

The above may seem obvious, but success depends on not ignoring problems, and not pretending that they don't exist.

Strategic planning tends to be optimistic when it moves away from known detail. The grass may all too often seem greener on the other side of the fence. This is where a carefully contructed merger between two parties is better than a blind bid, in that the aims of the acquiror can be tempered by the experience of the acquiree, who will probably tend to see the darker side of problems.

So far as possible, even with disputed bids, the aim should be to do a deal which will be equally fair and acceptable to both parties. If a merger is going to produce genuine benefits, there is surely room for generous terms for shareholders and employees on both sides. Clearly a clean and equitable deal is easier to live with; there should then be no cause for rancour or complaint to mar success.

Too little thought is sometimes given to whether a proposed merger, which seems logical and attractive from many points of view, is going to be compromised by existing loyalties and commercial ties. If commercial ties are important to the success of the merger, and if these are compromised by shortsightedness, or over-optimism in the proposal stage, the benefits from the merger could well be reduced; it is easy to believe that all will be right on the day and that there will be no problem. On the other hand, there is no need to be oversensitive; commercial ties tend to be rationally based and can stand a reasonable degree of strain. However, this is not true of loyalties where individuals are concerned. Most people have serious and emotionally based loyalties, which usually stem from various aspects of the individual's security and happiness. If people are important, and in virtually all mergers people are important, it is asking for trouble to make arrangements which do not take personal feelings into account.

### 6:12   Company image and good communications

A merger stands a better chance of success if the world in general and the Stock Market in particular thinks well of it. This may seem illogical, but the fact is that both individuals and organisations tend to work better in a harmonious environment.

Whether opinion approves or not will depend in part on the facts of the case, but also on how the facts are presented. In particular, it will depend on the balance given to the various pertinent facts. The careful management of public relations is very important.

The press should not be feared; instead, a good working relationship should be cultivated. If you help the press by giving time to ensuring that they are constructively briefed on what you are doing, or hoping to do, the press will help you in turn. To be uncooperative with the press is to invite antagonism.

Communications within and between the parties to a merger are important before and after the event. If the two sides in negotiations and planning do not understand each other, there will be trouble, while if the people representing each side do not have good communications with all parts of their respective companies, there will also be trouble.

### 6:13   Managing rationalisation and redundancy

The above is a guide to the pre-event factors which contribute materially to ultimate success. They can be summarised by saying that the commercial logic for the merger must be genuinely understood and must be right, and that people and their feelings are important and must be fully taken into account.

In the post-event phase, there is little that can be done about commercial logic as the die will have been cast, though it does matter how the "arrangements" are carried out. The consideration and handling of people become critical. Apart from the shareholders, who presumably will have been taken care of, the people we are really concerned with are the employees of the two companies. What is going to happen to these people?

A merger gives a unique opportunity to reappraise organisations in a way that would not be acceptable at other times. People will be expecting change and this is the time to institute not just the changes which stem directly from the merger, but all those other changes which management may well have considered desirable but rejected or shelved as being impractical or unacceptable at the time.

*Board and management changes.* Some of the first changes will probably be at board level. This is the time to retire, generously, those older directors who have already made their contributions to the growth of the business. This is the time to upgrade the men of the future. These moves are fairly critical in terms of making the merger a success, and although they need to be made at an early stage, the way should be left open for further changes to the board structure in the light of findings after, say, six months.

The aim should be to bring forward the better people and give them increased opportunity, so unlocking new talent and encouraging under-utilised talent. Individual board level changes may be facilitated by the need to alter board structures operationally, so that the personal effect of changes may be tempered.

Below board level, management changes will be needed to put the merger into effect and to rationalise after the event. Again, this is the time to reappraise management; it is also the time to break up existing rigid management structures and to replace them with flexible purpose-designed structures. This applies to both sides in a merger.

The best managers need to be brought forward to where their impact can be greatest. The more average managers need to be positioned so as to make the most of their perhaps limited talents, while the less able men need to be moved into positions where they will not impede the working of the system, or in certain cases, their services dispensed with altogether, though generously. The same rules hold for staff at lower levels.

The ideal is that no efficient employee should lose his or her job. In that mergers aim to create bigger and better enterprise, with more opportunities and therefore greater growth prospects, the outcome might be expected to mean more jobs for more people. But this is seldom the immediate case with either management and staff or labour.

The economies of size, and rationalisation, apart from the discontinuance of uneconomic or undesirable operations, may lead to redundancies which the expected short-term growth of the new business cannot absorb. A complication is that new jobs created by the merger may well not be geographically suitable or matched to the skills of the people made redundant.

Therefore there will be redundancies, and the success of the merger will be effected by how the matter is handled. The first rule is to avoid pretending that redundancies do not exist, and then to make the appropriate decisions with a determination to effect them. There are no firm rules for dealing with the people concerned, save to emphasise that people are naturally very sensitive when it comes to pride and personal security. Make the position clear as soon as possible, but avoid premature disclosure of decisions. Be informative and explain the background to decisions; be helpful, and be generous.

*Reorganisation.* Rationalisation must follow a merger. It is unreal to expect to merge two ideal companies on a wholly complementary basis. There will be some overlapping of both physical assets and people. Almost certainly new opportunities will be created which will need new organisations to exploit them, and there will be cases where uneconomic or perhaps uninspiring activities need to be curtailed or disposed of. In this there is wide opportunity for both success and failure.

Overall failure stems very often from failure to fully implement the planned changes for the post-merger phase. People may well find that they lack the courage of their earlier convictions. They may then be tempted to find doubtful reasons for not fully implementing their earlier plans. But a readiness to re-cast plans genuinely in the light of the actual post-merger situation is a factor in ultimate success. The benefits expected from a merger will not appear automatically. They will only be achieved through an active approach.

In reorganising there may be temptation to go for the neat solution, or for the politically acceptable solution. Neither should be altogether neglected, but to be over-motivated by these two factors could lead to a failure to realise the ultimately important commercial aims.

Both patience and the ability to press on are essential factors. Success and failure may well be determined by the balance of the two at any given time.

# SEVEN

# Financial Planning

*by Aris Presanis*

A company has two major financial problems which it must solve if it is to remain in business and prosper:

1  It must always have enough cash available to meet all its commitments as soon as they become due
2  Its business must be profitable

Even a profitable business can go bankrupt because it has insufficient cash to meet its commitments on the date due. Lack of profitability may not necessarily lead to immediate bankruptcy but lack of cash to meet commitments when due will almost certainly do so. A danger to be avoided is borrowing on a short term basis and using these funds for long term development except in those circumstances when arrangements have been made for re-financing temporary borrowings with more permanent finance. Such short term borrowings would then be called bridging finance, that is, moneys to bridge a short time gap between the date when money is spent for long term development and the date when money is received by raising permanent finance (see page 188).

Basically, profitability consists of spending £100 today to receive £110 by the end of a certain period of time. The accounting systems in use distinguish between spending for assets which are of a permanent nature (fixed assets, stocks, and so on) and other expenditure which is of a transient nature, such as salaries and rents. Because such distinctions are not always quite clear, the accounting profit figure can to a certain extent vary from year to year depending on management's accounting practices.

Both these problems are further complicated by the problem of time. The cash requirements of a company vary not only from month to month but also from year to year. Hence there may be times of excess cash and times of shortages, both within any one year and covering periods of years.

Equally important over the longer term are the trends and fluctuations of profits. Management of a company will no doubt want to be able to show a rising long term trend of profits as well as minimal year to year fluctuations.

## 7:1   Objectives of financial policy

From the above it is evident that there are two main objectives of financial policy:

1       To achieve an adequate growth of profits over a period of years with minimal year by year fluctuations
2       To maintain adequate cash to meet commitments when due and finance expansion where necessary, without retaining too much unprofitable spare cash at any one time.

*Profit growth and patterns.* In 1966 the author made a comparative study of the profitability of nine UK companies in the heavy chemical industry and ten companies in the pharmaceutical and toiletries industries. This study covered the years from 1956 and 1965 and it was found that over that period of time the average return on equity in both groups was exactly the same, i.e. $14\frac{3}{4}$ per cent a year after tax, but the profits in the heavy chemical group fluctuated more violently than those of the pharmaceutical and toiletry group as Table 7:1 shows.

In the case of the heavy chemicals the percentage of profits attributable to the equity increased by $2\frac{5}{8}$ per cent a year compound whereas that of the pharmaceutical and proprietaries group increased by only 2 per cent. Perhaps a ten year record may not be long enough to prove differences in trends, but this example is used simply to illustrate the fact that there are cases where management may wish to sacrifice more rapid growth of profits to a more stable pattern of profits or vice versa (see page 199).

| YEAR | AFTER TAX RETURN ON EQUITY EMPLOYED IN | |
| | HEAVY CHEMICALS | PHARMACEUTICALS AND TOILETRIES |
| --- | --- | --- |
| 1956 | 14.0 | 13.2 |
| 1957 | 13.1 | 13.6 |
| 1958 | 12.0 | 14.9 |
| 1959 | 15.6 | 15.5 |
| 1960 | 16.2 | 15.0 |
| 1961 | 13.5 | 14.0 |
| 1962 | 13.5 | 14.0 |
| 1963 | 15.0 | 14.3 |
| 1964 | 17.0 | 15.5 |
| 1965 | 18.3 | 16.0 |

TABLE 7:1 AVERAGE RETURN ON EQUITY IN NINE HEAVY CHEMICAL COMPANIES AND TEN PHARMACEUTICAL AND TOILETRY COMPANIES

*Relationship between profits and cash holding.* Whereas the return on the equity never fell below 12 per cent in either of the two groups mentioned in the previous paragraph, bank rate fluctuated during that period between a low of 4 per cent and a high of 7 per cent while the treasury bill rate fluctuated between a high of around $6\frac{1}{2}$ per cent and a low of $3\frac{1}{2}$ per cent. These last two rates were indicative of the return which could be obtained from surplus company cash invested in short term securities. Thus, loss of profits results from an accumulation of excess cash at any one time.

## 7:2 Estimating the company's cash flows

A company starts with a certain amount of cash which is used in various ways to produce eventually more cash than it started with. Basically an investment consists of spending cash now in the expectation of a series of cash flows in the future which not only will repay the original investment but will also produce more cash than originally invested. Hence, every investment which will involve the use of all sorts of resources—human and material—can be expressed in terms of cash. This statement is not intended to minimise the utility, the necessity, of human resources, including skilled management, but these will be expressed in terms of money when examined from a financial aspect. It therefore becomes essential to examine the way in which the cash flows of a company are estimated and following this to examine how best they can be used.

*Preparation of short-term forecast.* The cash flow forecast of a company can be of either short term (say a year ahead) or long term. The short term forecast serves to assess the liquidity of the company. Such a forecast should be of a "creeping" type and, depending on the type of business, should be reviewed regularly. A bank, for example, would build up daily for the next day whereas a business with regular receipts and payments would not need to revise such a forecast more often than once every three months. These cash forecasts should contain, on the receipts side:

1    Opening cash balance
2    Cash cales of products or services
3    Receipts from trade debtors
4    Income from investments (including rents, interest and dividends)
5    Receipts from other debtors
6    Receipts from new loans or subscriptions for shares
7    Refund of selective employment tax, if any
8    Refund of tax
9    Receipts from bank overdrafts, bills discounted, and so on
10   Receipts from sales of any fixed assets
11   Receipts of grants (investment, training and so on)

The expenditure side of the cash forecast should contain the following items:

1    Repayments of bank overdrafts or bills
2    Wages and salaries payable
3    Petty cash expenses
4    Payments for overhead expenditure (monthly, quarterly, half-yearly, yearly)
5    Payments to trade creditors for purchase of goods and services
6    Purchase tax payments, if any
7    Selective employment tax and other payments in respect of employees
8    Other tax payments
9    Interest and dividend payments
10   Payments for new fixed assets
11   Repayment for loans due
12   Payments for royalties, licence fees, and so on

*Preparation of long-term forecast.* When preparing a long term cash forecast it is obvious that detailed information as above would be meaningless. Furthermore the purpose of such a longer term forecast is different. While a short term forecast aims principally at making sure that there is enough cash in the kitty to meet current obligations which have been contracted and are or will shortly become due, the purpose of the longer term cash forecast is to enable a company to assess the amount of cash (in broad terms) which it will have available to finance its expansion. It is therefore possible to start from a different basis, as follows:

| | £ | |
|---|---|---|
| ESTIMATED SALES VALUE | | £ |
| Less materials | | |
| Labour | £ | |
| Overhead expenses | £ | |
| Rent if any | £ | |
| Purchase tax payments | £ | |
| Other indirect tax payments | £ | |
| Other expenses | £ | |
| Depreciation | £ | £ |
| | | |
| Gross profit before corporation tax | | £ |
| Less Interest payments if any | | £ |
| | | |
| Net profit before corporation tax | | £ |
| Less corporation tax | | £ |
| | | |
| Profit attributable to shareholders | | £ |
| Less Preferential dividend, if any | | £ |
| | | |
| Profit to ordinary shareholder | | £ |
| Less Dividend | | £ |
| | | |
| Retained earnings | | £ |
| Plus Depreciation | | £ |
| Net proceeds of sales of any assets | | £ |
| | | |
| *Total available for expansion* | | £ |

This is only an indication of the sort of items which should be included in such a long term cash forecast. Each business, however, must see that all significant items of current expenditure which may fluctuate independently are also shown separately. For example, if a commodity type raw material is a significant element in the cost of production, the cash forecast must show this separately, because fluctuations of its price will not necessarily coincide or in any way be similar to those of other materials. Also, certain significant elements of cost such as marketing expenses or expenses on transport of raw materials, semi-manufactured goods or finished products may also have to be shown separately. On the receipt side, it may be necessary to show details of volume and price as well as total value, because in some cases different combinations of sales would show up which is the most favourable to the company.

An important reason for separating the significant factors in building up the long term cash flow of a business is inflation. It is a well-known fact that the rates of inflation in prices, wages and so on are not uniform. Hence, it is necessary that separate inflationary factors should be applied to each significant element of a cash flow forecast, so that the total effect on the business can be more accurately assessed. For example, the speed with which increases in labour costs can be translated into increased prices is not the same in every industry and often the margin of profit is either squeezed or remains the same despite cost increases.

"Net proceeds of sales of any assets" in the cash flow forecast can be either a positive or negative figure and can represent fixed assets or working capital. If an item of fixed asset has been sold this may involve corporation tax on the basis of a "balancing charge or allowance" depending on whether the asset was sold at a price above or below its depreciated value for tax purposes. The figure which should be included is the net figure after taking into account any tax payable or receivable in connection with this transaction. Furthermore, any alteration in working capital, either as a result of a change in the volume or value of output or following changes in credit terms or for any other reason, should also be included in this item.

Finally, the cash flow forecast includes a figure for depreciation. This must of necessity be an estimate based not only on existing assets, which can be easily calculated, but also on any future expansion which preceded the year for which the cash flow has been prepared. This latter figure can only be an estimate based on the size and nature of the assets purchased. These would in most cases be of a similar nature to the existing assets and therefore a reasonable estimate of the depreciation figure can be included.

## 7:3   Example of cash flow table

There are various reasons for compiling a cash flow forecast. It gives an indication, for example, of the annual amount of cash available for expansion. This is necessary in order to see whether expansion can take place annually or whether cash must accumulate over a number of years before there is sufficient to finance a project of the size appropriate to the business the company is in. This aspect will be discussed in more detail later (see page 199).

The forecast also focuses the attention of management on the broad items of income and expenditure which have significant effect on the cash flow of the business and therefore on the proper employment of cash.

Let us use an example of a company which we have called the Midland Engineering Company Limited. It produces a variety of metalworking machine tools. During the last year the breakdown of the machine tools produced into the various costs of production and gross manufacturing margins was as follows:

| TYPE | 1 | 2 | 3 | 4 | 5 | 6 | 7 | 8 |
|---|---|---|---|---|---|---|---|---|
| *Centre lathes* | | | | | | | | |
| Sales price | £500 | 450 | 550 | 600 | 600 | 750 | | |
| Costs | | | | | | | | |
| Direct labour | 125 | 125 | 130 | 150 | 150 | 170 | | |
| Fuel materials | 220 | 230 | 220 | 375 | 195 | 355 | | |
| Maintenance | 50 | 50 | 50 | 50 | 50 | 50 | | |
| Packing and delivery | 10 | 10 | 10 | 10 | 10 | 10 | | |
| Total costs | 405 | 415 | 410 | 585 | 405 | 585 | | |
| Gross margin (per cent) | 19 | 8 | 25 | 2½ | 33 | 28 | | |
| *Milling machines* | | | | | | | | |
| Sales price | 1000 | 900 | 950 | 800 | 750 | 850 | | |
| Costs | | | | | | | | |
| Direct labour | 280 | 240 | 250 | 220 | 170 | 200 | | |
| Fuel and materials | 480 | 420 | 335 | 290 | 340 | 280 | | |
| Maintenance | 80 | 80 | 80 | 80 | 80 | 80 | | |
| Packing and delivery | 15 | 15 | 15 | 15 | 15 | 15 | | |
| Total costs | 855 | 755 | 680 | 605 | 605 | 575 | | |
| Gross margin (per cent) | 14 | 16 | 28 | 24 | 19 | 32 | | |
| *Radial drills* | | | | | | | | |
| Sales price | 1500 | 1250 | 1300 | 1400 | 1350 | 1250 | 1150 | 1150 |
| Costs | | | | | | | | |
| Direct labour | 350 | 200 | 200 | 225 | 225 | 300 | 275 | 200 |
| Fuel and materials | 400 | 350 | 350 | 250 | 250 | 450 | 425 | 250 |
| Maintenance | 100 | 100 | 100 | 100 | 100 | 100 | 100 | 100 |
| Packing and delivery | 20 | 20 | 20 | 20 | 20 | 20 | 20 | 20 |
| Total costs | 870 | 670 | 670 | 595 | 595 | 870 | 820 | 570 |
| Gross margin (per cent) | 45 | 46 | 48 | 58 | 36 | 30 | 29 | 50 |

| TYPE | 1 | 2 | 3 | 4 | 5 | 6 | 7 | 8 |
|---|---|---|---|---|---|---|---|---|
| *Presses* | | | | | | | | |
| Sales price | £7000 | 5500 | 4000 | 6000 | 5000 | | | |
| Costs | | | | | | | | |
|   Direct labour | 1100 | 1050 | 800 | 1000 | 950 | | | |
|   Fuel and materials | 1700 | 1650 | 1400 | 1700 | 1650 | | | |
|   Maintenance | 200 | 200 | 200 | 200 | 200 | | | |
|   Packing and delivery | 25 | 25 | 25 | 25 | 25 | | | |
| Total costs | 3025 | 2925 | 2425 | 2925 | 2825 | | | |
| Gross margin (per cent) | 57 | 47 | 39 | 51 | 43 | | | |

The cash flow of the company during the same year was as follows:

| | (£'000) | | | % |
|---|---|---|---|---|
| Sales proceeds | £12 780 | | | 100.0 |
| Less costs of production | 8 130 | | | 63.5 |
| Gross manufacturing margin | | £4 650 | | 36.5 |
| Less:  Factory overheads | 875 | | 6.8 | |
|        Sales and marketing costs | 1 075 | | 8.4 | |
|        Research and development | 75 | | .6 | |
|        HQ administration | 490 | 2 515 | 3.9 | 19.7 |
| Trading profit before tax and depreciation | | 2 135 | | 16.8 |
| Plus interest on investments | | 400 | | 3.1 |
| Total profit before tax and depreciation | | 2 535 | | 19.9 |
| Less:  Depreciation | 350 | | 2.7 | |
|        Corporation tax on previous year's profits paid this year (at 45% rate) | 800 | 1 150 | 6.3 | 9.0 |
| Profit to ordinary shareholders | | 1 385 | | 10.9 |
| Less dividend paid during year (20%) | | 1 000 | | |
| Retained earnings | | 385 | | |
| Plus depreciation | 350 | | | |
| Asset changes | | | | |
|   Reduction in working capital | 415 | | | |
|   Investment grants received | 100 | 865 | | |
| Total increase in cash | | 1 250 | | |
| Plus cash available from previous year | | 2 690 | | |
| Total cash available end 1970 | | £3 940 | | |

The balance sheet of this company at the end of 1970 was as follows (in £'000):

|  | COST | DEPRECIATION | NET |
|---|---|---|---|
| Land and buildings | £5 000 | £3 125 | £1 875 |
| Plant and machinery | 10 000 | 9 095 | 905 |
| Total | 15 000 | 12 220 | 2 780 |

| Current Assets: Stocks | £2 960 | | |
|---|---|---|---|
| Debtors | 3 045 | | |
| Cash | 3 940 | | |
|  |  | £9 945 | |
| Current liabilities: Trade creditors | £1 540 | | |
| Tax payable next year (at 42½% rate) | 930 | | |
| Dividend payable | 600 | £3 070 | £6 875 |
| Total assets | | | £9 655 |

| Represented by: 5 000 000 ordinary £1 | | |
|---|---|---|
| shares | | £5 000 |
| Capital reserves | | 2 500 |
| Revenue reserves | | 2 000 |
| Profit and loss account | | 155 |
| Total | | £9 655 |

There is a footnote to the accounts that a recent valuation of the company's fixed assets made by professional valuers has assessed the value of land and buildings at £5 500 000 and the plant and machinery at £2 000 000 making a total of £7 500 000 against their book value of £2 780 000.

## 7:4 Interpreting the cash flow table

An important factor which appears from the cash flow table is that the overall gross manufacturing margin on total sales proceeds is only 36½ per cent and this should be compared with the GMM of individual products and lines which is as follows:

| | MAXIMUM % | MINIMUM % | AVERAGE % |
|---|---|---|---|
| Centre lathes | 33 (type 5) | 2½ (type 4) | 18½ |
| Milling machines | 32 (type 6) | 14 (type 1) | 22½ |
| Radial drills | 58 (type 4) | 29 (type 7) | 45½ |
| Presses | 57 (type 1) | 39 (type 3) | 45 |

Another interesting factor arising from a careful examination of the cash flow table is that profit accruing to the shareholders is less than 11 per cent of sales, of which interest on investments represents about 3 per cent.

If a series of cash flows from the previous years were examined some further interesting lessons could be learned, such as a high labour element in the manufacturing process but low fuel and materials cost. This would indicate a substantial amount of hand labour and little mechanisation of production or subcontracting. Perhaps more mechanisation and possibly some sub-contracting of parts which could not easily be produced by more mechanised methods would be more profitable than the present system of operations.

On the overheads structure it would seem that the total is high at about 20 per cent of sales while the amount used for research and development at 0.6 per cent seems too low. Perhaps this is why no new and more economical methods of production were developed.

On the subject of working capital, some interesting points may be raised. Stocks represent 36½ per cent of annual sales at production cost, that is, they represent over four months' sales. Considering that the average production time in the industry is only four weeks, this stock level might be considered high. An assessment of the right stock level could be made on the following basis:

**1**  *Materials.* Total used during 1970 equals £4 680 000, that is approximately £400 000 a month. Depending on the ease of obtaining materials from the suppliers on request, it may appear prudent to hold one month's requirements in stock, that is, £400 000.

**2**  *Work in progress.* This would require one month's materials (£400 000), plus on average fifteen days' direct labour costs (approximately £75 000)—say a total of not more than £500 000.

**3**  *Finished products.* As obviously some of the products are stock items, it follows that this would be more difficult to control. However, a minimum stockholding of one month's sales (£750 000) or a maximum of two months' sales (£1 500 000) should be aimed at. It should be possible to adjust production schedules within these limits.

From the above discussion it is obvious that stocks should be lower and should fluctuate between a minimum of £1 700 000 and a maximum of £2 400 000 and that the present figure of £2 960 000 is too high for the present levels of sales. The aim of policy should therefore be to reduce it by between £750 000 and £1 000 000, thus releasing some cash for other uses.

Debtors at £3 045 000 represent about three months' sales, so it seems that the company is giving three months' credit to its customers. The decision on the length of credit to be given is a policy decision and must be taken at high level after consultation with the marketing and finance functions of the company. A halving of the credit terms from three months to six weeks would release some £1 500 000 of extra cash which could be used in other parts of the business. Such a decision would have to be weighed against possible loss of sales and, more important, whether such sales are in products which at present give adequate profit margins or whether they are concentrated on the low priced low profit products.

Trade creditors at £1 540 000, representing about three to four months' purchases of materials, fuel, maintenance and packaging supplies, appear favourable to the company. However some cash should be held in reserve in case suppliers also decided to shorten the period of credit they are prepared to give. This could well be reduced by half, which would require some £750 000 additional cash. The likelihood of such an eventuality should be carefully considered by the finance functions and provision should be made, if necessary, in the firm's cash forecasts.

Finally, it should be noted that between 40 and 50 per cent of total direct production costs represent labour (including the labour element in maintenance and factory overheads) and it may be considered that this is too high. Studies should be made to find out ways of reducing this cost, either by using more power, or by better product design, or better organisation of production runs, or even better layout of the factory space. This question of a more effective utilisation of labour is extremely important for two reasons:

1    Technically qualified labour is and will remain one of the
     most scarce resources of the country

2        Wages must be expected to rise both in real and in money
         terms over the years owing to the increased bargaining
         strength of trade unions

From the above discussion certain conclusions can be drawn. The cash
flow studies have shown that the company has available from internal
sources considerable cash resources over and above what is shown in
the balance sheet, as follows:

1  *Working capital.* Reduction in stocks      (say)    £900 000
                      Reduction in debtors      (say)  £1 500 000
                                                       ───────────

                      Total                             £2 400 000
               Less increase in trade creditors   £750 000
                                                       ───────────

                      Total additional cash            £1 650 000
                                                       ───────────

2  *Fixed assets.* The hidden value of these is of the order of £4 700 000
(the difference between their present market value and their book value).
How much a difference could be realised is discussed later (see page 188).
3  *Running costs* could be reduced by rationalising the range of products
made and the method of manufacturing them. The finance function is
not responsible for saying how this should be done but should indicate
the need for action. Furthermore, the finance function should point out
the high level of overhead expenditure within the organisation and
particularly in the factory and headquarters administration and the
marketing and sales function. It may also wish to query the policy
which keeps expenditure on research and development at such a low
level.

Financial policy consists of comparing the possible alternative returns
resulting from the use of cash. Basically, the cost of the money used in
any one particular project is the profit or return the company has
foregone by not using that money in the most profitable alternative way
and not what the company pays as a dividend to shareholders or as
interest to lenders. This is what economists call the opportunity cost of
money. This concept will become clearer in the example of the Midland
Engineering Company Limited already mentioned. If, as a result of the
cash saving operations already mentioned (see page 181), the company

raised an additional £1 500 000 by tightening credit and if as a result sales fell by about 10 per cent (say £1 250 000) and this was spread equally throughout the whole range of products, then profits before tax would be reduced by about £450 000 (36½ per cent of £1 250 000). It follows that the cost of raising the £1 500 000 would in such an event be 30 per cent before tax. If however, the fall in sales was concentrated only on the low profit margin products then the reduction in profits before tax could be as low as £125 000 (10 per cent of £1 250 000) or 8.3 per cent on £1 500 000 before tax. Assuming that this money could be placed in the market at 9 per cent, the opportunity cost of this saving in working capital would be 9 per cent before tax because this latter is the higher figure.

This concept of opportunity cost is very important when assessing the value to a company of alternative uses of funds. Later in this chapter techniques for assessing the use of funds on a comparable basis will be outlined.

## 7:5   Nature of the company's capital

The money used in a business (its capital) comes from two sources—the shareholders and the various persons who lent money to this business. There are two ways in which this capital can be divided:

**1**   Permanent capital and loan capital
(*a*) The permanent capital belongs to the shareholders (ordinary or preference), who are the real owners of a business. This becomes repayable only on the liquidation of a business.
(*b*) The loan capital is a claim in monetary terms by a lender to the business. This capital is not permanent because it is due for repayment on specified contractual dates.
**2**   Equity capital and fixed interest capital
(*a*)   Equity belongs to the ordinary shareholders and the dividend is not contractually fixed but varies according to the level of profits and the board's distribution policy.
(*b*)   Fixed interest capital bears contractually agreed interest or dividend, whether it is loan capital or preference shares.

In view of the effects of inflation on profits and interest payments the second distinction seems more useful and is used in this chapter. In the context of this distinction, equity represents the shareholders' interest in the company, carrying the main risks and benefiting from all profits after expenses and interest. It usually takes the form of ordinary shares with a nominal value (in the USA, ordinary or common shares can be issued with no par value but this is not allowed in the UK). This nominal value usually bears little relation to either their book value or their market value. In the example of the Midland Engineering Company Limited, the nominal value of the shares is £1 each, the book value is £1.92 and on a price earnings basis of say 10 the shares could have a market value of say £2.42. The price earnings ratio of a share is calculated by the following formula:

$$\text{Price earnings} = \frac{\text{Price a share}}{\text{After Corporation Tax earnings per share}}$$

If the price earnings ratio was 16 then the share price would be £3.87. More about the market valuation of shares will be said later (page 191).

Fixed interest capital can take various forms, depending on the risk involved and the length of the commitment of the investor. Basically, preference shares are part of the risk capital of a company and often are irredeemable except through liquidation of the company. However the interest paid on them is fixed and for the purpose of financial planning should be considered as fixed interest capital although they are treated differently from loan capital for tax purposes.

Loan stocks are straightforward borrowings of the company for a specific length of time at a specific rate of interest. Such loans may be secured by a debenture on specified assets of the company or by a general floating charge on all assets (after any debentures on specified assets have been satisfied) or be unsecured. These are all long term liabilities probably of 20 to 25 years' duration.

At times preference or loan stocks have attached to them the right at the option of the holder to convert part or all of his holding into ordinary shares at specified terms on specified dates. Alternatively they may have warrants attached giving the holder the option to buy a certain number of new ordinary shares at a specified price on a specified date.

Finally the company can obtain capital to cover temporary requirements or shorter term requirements from banks, merchant banks or finance houses.

## 7:6  Gearing of company capital

Usually the cost of raising capital in the form of borrowing is cheaper than raising it in the form of equity; hence there is a tendency to prefer to raise as much as is *safely* possible in the form of borrowings. Again the question of cash comes in, because the company should always be in a position to meet interest and capital repayments on maturity. The proportion between prior capital (fixed interest capital) and equity depends on the type of business. Some general guiding rules may be given here.

A company with large fixed assets, small working capital, steady profits and low profit margin in relation to sales can have as much as 70 per cent prior capital. Examples of this are utilities and property companies.

A company with small fixed assets or fixed assets which can be used only for a specific purpose, large working capital, violently fluctuating profits and profit margins should not have as much prior capital. Examples of this are industrial companies making heavy capital goods, machine tools or chemicals.

The ratio of equity to total capital is called gearing. A company is said to have a high gearing when the proportion of equity to total is low and the converse (low gearing) when it is high.

The normal gearing now acceptable in the UK for the average industrial company is approximately 70 per cent equity to 30 per cent fixed interest capital. The Midland Engineering Company Limited has no fixed interest capital and according to the rule of thumb set out above, could raise an additional £4 000 000 or so, thus raising its gearing to the more normal 70/30 ratio.

## 7:7 Influence of government on company finance

The government's contribution to company finance is a very complex operation because money between government and business flows both ways. Assume a business wants to start a new project in some particular part of the country and must start by buying land. Planning permission for this must be given and the owner of the land will probably have to pay a betterment levy. As soon as the company starts employing people it will have to pay a training levy to the industry's training board but it can also claim from them all or part of the cost of training them. It must also pay selective employment tax on all its employees and can reclaim this in certain cases with, sometimes, a further premium. The company must pay corporation tax on any profits made after certain allowances for wear and tear of its productive equipment. If it pays any dividend it must retain income tax which it then pays to the Inland Revenue. Until recently a company could also claim

| YEAR | COMPANY RETENTIONS INCLUDING DEPRECIATION | OTHER SOURCES (1) | NEW SHARE AND LOAN CAPITAL | | | | NEW MONEY TOTAL |
|---|---|---|---|---|---|---|---|
| | | | ORDINARY | PREFERENCE | LONG TERM LOAN | BANK LOANS | |
| 1954 | 767 | 235 | 65 | 24 | 86 | 29 | 1206 |
| 5 | 833 | 264 | 157 | 29 | 83 | 65 | 1431 |
| 6 | 822 | 207 | 161 | 9 | 112 | 78 | 1380 |
| 7 | 879 | 176 | 245 | 28 | 154 | 52 | 1534 |
| 8 | 914 | 87 | 159 | 11 | 85 | 18 | 1274 |
| 9 | 1142 | 289 | 263 | 19 | 70 | 68 | 1851 |
| 1960(2) | 1171 | 412 | 414 | 27 | 27 | 149 | 2200 |
| 1 | 1016 | 265 | 491 | 16 | 105 | 175 | 2068 |
| 2 | 1058 | 215 | 269 | 31 | 299 | 78 | 1950 |
| 3 | 1290 | 457 | 208 | 20 | 165 | 120 | 2260 |
| 4(3) | 1574 | 607 | 295 | 30 | 220 | 187 | 2913 |
| 5 | 1707 | 548 | 265 | 9 | 377 | 339 | 3245 |
| 6 | 1416 | 310 | 269 | −77 | 565 | 210 | 2693 |
| 7(4) | 1404 | 413 | 59 | −20 | 422 | 50 | 2328 |
| 8(4) | 955 | 518 | 211 | −49 | 196 | 190 | 2021 |

(1) Mainly increase in creditors (trade and other) and sale of assets.
(2) In 1960 there was a revision of the allocation of funds as between certain groups.
(3) In 1964 there was a further revision of the allocation of funds as between certain groups.
(4) The amounts shown in 1967 and 1968 are provisional.

TABLE 7:2 SOURCES OF FINANCE OF QUOTED COMPANIES

Source: *Annual Abstract of Statistics and Financial Statistics*

from the government investment grants in part refund of certain capital expenditures. This has recently been abolished, with accelerated depreciation taking its place. Specialists within a company should study these transfers insofar as they affect the particular circumstances of the company and should keep abreast of any changes which may take place annually at the time of the budget and sometimes more often.

As most of these taxes and grants will relate to specific projects or operations of a company they must be examined in relation to the cash flows of this specific project or operation because their effect on the company's cash outlay and profitability can be substantial. For example, a company can depreciate for tax purposes the full value of an investment in plant and machinery in a development area within the year it has been paid; some repayments of selective employment tax can be worth as much as two hours' work a week for certain categories of workers.

### 7:8 Raising short-term finance

The importance of the sources of outside finance must not be overlooked. Table 7:2, compiled by the Department of Trade and Industry shows that of the total new money raised annually by quoted industrial and commercial companies with capital in excess of £500 000 and profits in excess of £50 000 some two-thirds comes from internal sources, mainly retained earnings and depreciation but also sale of assets, and the remaining third from external sources, including bank loans.

A short discussion of the mechanics of raising outside finance is necessary. The form of raising money depends on whether the moneys are required to finance short or long term requirements. Short term finance may be obtained from a banker (bank overdraft), an acceptance house (acceptance credit), or a hire purchase finance company. Intermediate and long term finance can be obtained from a hire purchase company, from a government-sponsored financial corporation, from an insurance company or from the market. Equity finance can be obtained from existing shareholders, from shareholders of other businesses by exchanging their shares in that business for shares in the purchasing business, from a new partner and from the market.

A banker or an acceptance house wants to make sure that the borrower's financial standing is adequate to cover the loan, that is, that his free assets (not charged in any other way) are a sufficiently large security for the amount of the loan and, more important, that the expected cash flow of the business will be adequate to maintain all payments, including repayments of the loan when these become due.

As both these forms of borrowing are essentially short term they are appropriate to cover self-liquidating transactions such as seasonal variations in trade and special purchase of goods for resale, probably after processing, where the purchases and sales are matched.

*Obtaining bridging finance.* If a company is undertaking a major project of expansion for which more permanent capital is due to be raised later, some short term borrowing from bankers or an acceptance house could be arranged to bridge such a gap (bridging loan). These bridging loans can have a very wide application. For example, if a firm is buying another which has large hidden resources it could borrow part of the purchase price from a merchant bank and repay them when it has completed the purchase and got control of the assets of the acquired company. The Midland Engineering Company Limited has cash of approximately £4 000 000, possibly excess working capital of say £1 500 000, and hidden reserves of approximately £4 500 000, making a total of £10 000 000. A purchaser of this company for £10 000 000 (£2 a share) would be able to raise that amount in cash once he obtained control. He could therefore use a merchant bank to raise £10 000 000 to finance his purchase.

Alternatively if Midland Engineering Company Limited wanted to spend, say, £10 000 000 on moving its factories to a new site it could raise the missing £4 500 000 (£10 000 000 less £4 000 000 existing cash and £1 500 000 excess working capital) by selling the old factories for approximately £7 500 000 once the new factories are operational. This is one way of realising the hidden value of the company's fixed assets— a method that has also the advantage of replacing older buildings and machinery with modern assets. Another way is by the sale of these assets to a property firm and then leasing them back. In this way Midland Engineering would receive cash now against a series of cash payments extending over the years.

This method is recommended only if the company can earn more on the cash it will be receiving than it will be paying in leasehold rent over the years. It should also be appreciated that a property company will only buy the land and buildings—not the plant and machinery—so that Midland Engineering would only raise £5 500 000 in this way and not the full £7 500 000.

*Overdrafts and acceptance credits.* Banks and merchant banks use different methods of lending money. The simplest is the overdraft. More complex is the acceptance credit. This consists of a line of credit based on a sale of goods for which a bill of exchange is issued. Basically the transaction consists of firm $A$ selling goods to firm $B$. Firm $A$ (the drawer) draws a bill on firm $B$ (the payee) which it presents to firm $B$'s merchant bank (the acceptor) who accepts it on behalf of the payee. There are complex legal regulations and requirements about the respective rights of the various parties but from the corporate finance point of view two features are important:

1 Overdrafts are more flexible, both in relation to the timing of the borrowing (because the firm uses them only as and when needed and for the exact time it needs them) and as regards interest rates, which may vary each time bank rate changes.
2 Acceptance credits are fixed by the "tenor" of the bill, that is, they are usually 90 days, 120 days and exceptionally 180 days, so that the borrowing is for a "fixed" term, albeit short. Furthermore, the cost of an acceptance credit is threefold: a fixed commitment commission which is charged when the line of credit is agreed between the merchant bank and the firm, a further fixed charge on each bill when accepted (acceptance commission) and an interest rate to discount the bill if the firm wants the cash immediately.

Despite the relative inflexibility of acceptance credits as against overdrafts they have their use as a source of finance if, for example, the buyer and seller are in different countries and do not know each other well, or as an additional source of finance when credit restrictions make bank overdrafts difficult to obtain. Firms can also finance their basic working capital requirements by acceptance credits and leave overdrafts to finance the marginal fluctuating requirements.

*Hire purchase transactions.* Just as property companies purchase land and buildings and then lease them to the user on long term, so hire purchase companies purchase machinery, vehicles and other medium life assets and lease them or sell them on hire purchase terms to users. For the industrial user there are differences between leasing and hire purchasing. When leasing, the ownership of the goods remains with the lessor and the goods revert to him after the termination of the lease. With hire purchasing, the goods, on completion of the hire purchase payments, become the full property of the user. This difference in the legal ownership is important in estimating the cost of the asset because it involves differences in the treatment of the rental/hire charge for tax purposes, of the investment grant and of the residual value of the asset.

The rate of interest charged on a hire purchase transaction is usually expressed as a percentage of the total amount borrowed (say 10 per cent a year) but the repayments could be monthly. If the transaction covers three years the interest added would be 3 times 10 per cent. The true rate of interest would then be much higher (in this instance $17\frac{3}{4}$ per cent a year) and can be found by the following equations [see paragraph 6:18 for derivation of true rate of compound interest on a hire purchase transaction]:

$$\text{True rate of interest} = \frac{200 \times M \times D}{P(n+1) + 1/3\, D(n-1)}$$

where M is the number of payments in a full year (say 12 monthly payments)

    D is the total amount paid less the amount borrowed

    P is the amount borrowed

    n is the total number of payments needed to discharge the debt

## 7:9   Raising long-term finance

Longer term or permanent capital is broadly divided into equity—which is permanent—and loan, which is long term but has to be repaid on a specified date. In between is preference capital which can be either long term or permanent depending on the terms of issue. Public companies (those whose shares are owned by the general public) usually raise such funds through the capital market. This rather nebulous concept consists of all the institutions and private individuals who have money to invest and all the institutions and companies which require money to run and expand their business over and above the money they can generate internally. This demand and supply situation meets in the stock exchanges, of which there are a number in the UK. The most important of these is the London Stock Exchange. There are some 9500 securities quoted on the London Stock Exchange, valued at over £100 000 million. Of these securities some 8300 belong to some 4000 public companies, 90 per cent of which are registered and managed in the UK. There are some 2300 companies included in the general category of "commercial, industrial, etc" and their quoted capital is valued as follows:

|  | £ million |
|---|---:|
| Loan capital | 2 000 |
| Preference and preferred capital | 599 |
| Ordinary and deferred capital | 19 658 |
| Total | £22 257 |

Securities of other companies including those of companies not registered or managed in the UK are valued at £60 000 million and British and Overseas Government stock another £20 500 million.

All the above figures are as at 29 March 1968 (*Stock Exchange Year Book* 1969).

*Effect of share prices.* The prices of individual shares fluctuate considerably in the short term as a result of rumours, expectations of take-overs and the general political and economic climate, but by and large reflect the opinion of the value of capital in the company concerned, including not only the dividend at present paid on these shares but also the expectation of profits to be earned in the future. The price of the shares of a company is therefore a measure of its performance.

General political and economic factors also affect prices but, usually, this affects all shares in a similar manner (upward or downward). Company managements should watch the trend of the price of their own company's share and compare this with the general market trend and the trend in the price of shares in other similar companies. Investors tend to sell shares in companies with poor prospects and buy shares in companies with better prospects, so that over the longer term some shares give a higher dividend yield whereas others give a lower yield. If however a discounted cash flow yield was calculated over that long period, taking into account rises in dividends and in the price of shares it would be found that the DCF return on both types of shares was similar, the lack of growth being compensated by the high original yield. A calculation of the rate of return to shareholders for the seven groups of equities included in the *Financial Times*/Institute of Actuaries Shares Index was made covering the years 1950 to 1965 (see *Corporate Planning in Industry* by A Presanis). This gave a DCF rate of return (after tax) to shareholders as follows:

| GROUP | RATE OF RETURN % |
|---|---|
| All shares index | $9\frac{1}{2}$ |
| Capital goods shares index | $9\frac{1}{2}$ |
| Chemicals shares index | $11\frac{1}{4}$ |
| Non-durable consumer goods shares index | $9\frac{3}{4}$ |
| Oil shares index | $16\frac{1}{4}$ |
| Shipping shares index | $7\frac{3}{4}$ |
| Financial shares index | $11\frac{1}{2}$ |

These returns were based both on dividends paid during the period and on capital appreciation; they have not been deflated by the fall in the value of money.

Since 1965 the political and economic climate in which private industry operates in the UK has deteriorated with the double taxation of profits (corporation tax) and dividends (income tax) with rising labour costs (including selective employment tax and National Insurance contributions) and finally rise in interest rates which makes borrowings more expensive. Prices have also risen but the rise in prices seems to follow rather than precede the rise in costs which tends to narrow margins. This increase in production costs applies to all developed economies but the squeeze on profits seems to be more intense in the UK because the rise in productivity is generally slower there than overseas.

It follows that, although managements may aim to achieve at least similar growth in the future as in the past, external influences might well prevent them from doing so. However as individual performance is measured relatively to that of the group, management's aim should be to perform at least as well as its own group and as the "all shares" group—if not better. Hence, if the aim of Midland Engineering is to achieve say 11 per cent DCF return for its shareholders ($1\frac{1}{2}$ per cent above the average for the capital goods share in the past and $1\frac{1}{2}$ per cent above the average of all shares) but it only achieves say 8 per cent because of external circumstances which have lowered the average to $6\frac{1}{2}$ per cent (from $9\frac{1}{2}$ per cent), then their relative performance is as good as (or even slightly better than) originally planned. It should be pointed out that a shareholder holding a negotiable instrument (a share quoted on a stock exchange) will buy or sell the share and eventually move the price in such a manner that ultimately its yield will approximate to that of the average. In fact, if a company's profits are growing rapidly, a larger proportion of the DCF return to shareholders consists of the capital growth element and a smaller proportion of the dividend yield. The converse happens with shares in companies which show a small growth or static long term earnings growth.

*Long-term loans.* Long term loan capital is the cheapest form of finance because the interest is allowable for corporation tax purpose. Loan capital can take the form of a secured debenture or an unsecured loan stock. The former are secured under a trust deed on all or on specified assets of the company which the company cannot dispose of without the specific authority of the trustees. However when the debenture is on all assets of the company there is a clause permitting the company to dispose of assets in the ordinary course of business. When debentures are issued by a company the market will require that the value of the assets of the company after the debenture is raised should cover the amount received at least three times and that the interest on the debenture should be covered at least four times by the average of the profits of the preceding four years. Managements should be careful when raising a secured debenture that the restrictions on further borrowings imposed are flexible so that, as the assets and profits of the company grow (through retained earnings, new issues of shares, and so on), the possibility of further borrowings is not excluded, as it would be if all the assets were charged with no provision of a formula for further borrowings.

Unsecured loan stock is more flexible and could be marginally more expensive than a secured debenture. Although in this type of loan the assets are not charged, the market will probably watch that the company does not overborrow and will be using a similar formula for its assessment. It should also be pointed out that such unsecured loans are usually available only to the larger companies.

Preference shares are at present a dying breed. The law considers them as part of the risk capital of a company but not part of the equity. They rank in front of the ordinary shares for capital and interest and usually have no further interest in the equity. They are usually irredeemable (but not always) and therefore have no value as an inflation hedge and no hope of participating in the growth of profits of the company. In fact they differ little from borrowings, ranking last in the event of the company getting into difficulties. On the other hand corporation tax legislation treats them as part of the company's capital and therefore the dividend (or interest) on preference shares is paid to the shareholder from profits which have been subjected to corporation tax. It follows that to pay a $5\frac{1}{2}$ per cent dividend to preference shareholders is equivalent to paying a 10 per cent dividend to loan stock holders when corporation tax is at 45 per cent. Many a company has therefore found it profitable to convert old irredeemable preference stock to new redeemable loan stock at a slightly higher interest rate and of course the preference shareholders will then get a higher interest rate as well as a promise to get their money back at a certain fixed date.

## 7:10   Cost of raising external finance

The present net cost to a company of raising finance from outside sources can be listed as follows (the cost is net of corporation tax at 45 per cent where applicable):

*Type of finance*

|  | | % Cost |
|---|---|---|
| 1 | Bank overdraft—the most flexible form of finance but basically short term with possibilities of periodical renewals | $4\frac{1}{2}$ to $5\frac{1}{2}$ |
| 2 | Acceptance credit—less flexible, usable under certain conditions of an underlying self-liquidating transaction in goods for a stated short term period of 90 or 120 or 180 days | 5 to 6 |
| 3 | Sale and lease back of land and buildings | up to 8 |
| 4 | Hire purchase of plant and machinery, vehicles and so on | 8 to 12 |
| 5 | Long-term loans—depending on the form these take | 6 to 8 |
| 6 | Preference shares—there is no relief of corporation tax on their dividend | 9 to 11 |
| 7 | Equity—the cost of these would depend on market conditions and would be somewhere between | 8 and 12 |

## 7:11   Profit planning objectives

Profit should be the prime objective of a company. The profit objective must be quantified because such expressions as maximising profit in the short term or maximising net present value of shares or any such other definition is meaningless to management. For management a meaningful expression of profits is either return on capital employed (return on investment) or return on sales (sales margin). These are figures that management easily understands and are certainly quantifiable. Nevertheless the relationship between the board of a company and its shareholders should also be a major consideration. Ultimately, unless shareholders receive a satisfactory return on their shares the board will lose their support. This can either take the form of a drop in the value of the shares or a take-over operation by some other company. Neither situation is comfortable for management.

A shareholder owning ordinary shares in a particular company expects a certain return on his investment. This return consists of two parts:

1  The dividend which he is now receiving
2  The capital appreciation (or the increase in dividends which he expects to receive over the next few years)

The return is decided by the stock market, which places a price on the shares of a company commensurate to the past performance in terms of profits and dividends and future expectations.

The board therefore has very little option other than deciding that their objective is to achieve a certain rate of growth of earnings a share at least equal to that of the average of all industry and maybe more in certain industries which are more favourably placed. This would imply a DCF rate of return to shareholders of around 10 per cent or more depending on the industry.

The next point the board must decide is how much dividend they intend to pay and what proportion of earnings they intend to retain, that is, the distribution share of the cake. This decision has no long term effect on the market price of the shares or on the rate of return to shareholders but it is a necessary planning decision, as we shall see later on (see page 196).

The rate of growth of profits of the company and the proportion of profits retained bring into consideration the time factor. It is, of course, much more difficult to double a company's profits in five years than to double them in twenty years. To illustrate this point, if the board wants to double the company's profits over five years the rate of increase a year is $12\frac{1}{2}$ per cent—if they want to do it in seven years it is 10 per cent, in ten years, $7\frac{1}{2}$ per cent and in twenty years $3\frac{1}{2}$ per cent. Hence the time scale of planning becomes important.

Another board decision required in this planning operation is the level of gearing that the company should have.

## 7:12    Making profit planning decisions

The board should start the profit planning operation by taking the following basic decisions:

1    The rate of growth of profits per share the company should aim at
2    The proportion of profits per share which will be distributed as dividends
3    The ideal gearing of the company's capital structure

These objectives, however, are meaningless to line management and they have to be translated into return on capital employed and/or margin on sales.

*Profits as return on capital employed.* The first stage is to translate the required profits into return on capital employed. This is a mathematical operation which involves forecasting the cash flows on the basis of the present business of the company and assuming that any excess cash is reinvested in the business to earn a return which will achieve the required growth of profit. A mathematical formula is drawn up which is solved for the rate of interest. It implies a simulation exercise of the company and can be done by the company's OR department or by a consultant if the company does not have an OR department.

It will be found that any long term improvement in present returns on capital employed can only be made either by reducing costs or by new investment. Often, reducing costs implies a new investment. If it does not, then it means that management has not been operating existing investment as profitably as it should have been. Raising prices, except as a last resort, is an operation of doubtful value. A new investment can be achieved only if cash is available and the cash resources that will be accruing to the company are:

1    Depreciation
2    Retained earnings
3    New prior capital, such as new loans

For the purpose of this exercise the possibility of new equity capital is ignored at this stage.

Earlier, the proportion of earnings which should be retained was mentioned as a major policy decision. This decision becomes important at this stage because a higher proportion of retained earnings means higher cash availability for new investment and therefore renders much easier management's effort to achieve a certain level of earnings. The total cash availability is then related to the absolute level of earnings it is the board's aim to achieve and this gives a management objective of return on capital. From then on individual divisional or functional management objectives are determined.

*Expressing financial objectives in management terms.* An illustration from Midland Engineering Company Limited is useful. Let us assume that the board took the following planning decisions:

1    That over the next five years profits to equity should be doubled from about £1 400 000 to £2 800 000, implying a rate of growth of $12\frac{1}{2}$ per cent

2      That by the end of the five-year period dividends should
       be increased to £1 500 000 (30 per cent) from the present
       £1 000 000 (20 per cent)
3      That the company at an appropriate time would raise loan
       capital of up to 30 per cent of its total capital employed

To achieve this result the company has available the following resources:

| | |
|---|---|
| Cash in hand | £3 500 000 |
| Excess working capital | £1 500 000 |
| Possible borrowing 30 per cent of total capital employed | |
| which after a revaluation of fixed assets would amount to | |
| approx. £14 000 000 | £4 300 000 |
| Total | £8 300 000 |

To this must be added the cash accruing annually to the company from retained earnings and depreciation. A simulation exercise could be carried out based on various assumptions of annual profitability and profit retentions as well as cash from depreciation provisions. In say five years' time some £4 700 000 of additional profits before tax, depreciation and interest on new capital would be required to achieve the profit objective. The profit and loss account would then look as follows:

| | | |
|---|---|---|
| Trading profit on old business (see page 178) | | £2 100 000 |
| Additional profit on new business | | 4 700 000 |
| Total trading profit | | £6 800 000 |
| Less: Depreciation on old business | £350 000 | |
| Depreciation on new business say: | | |
| 15 per cent on £6 000 000 plant and | | |
| machinery | £900 000 | |
| 4 per cent on £2 000 000 building | £80 000 | £1 330 000 |
| Gross profit | | £5 470 000 |
| Less: Interest on new loan of £4 300 000 at say | | |
| 11 per cent a year | | 470 000 |
| Net profit to equity before tax | | 5 000 000 |
| Less: Corporation tax at $42\frac{1}{2}$ per cent | | 2 125 000 |
| Net after tax profit to equity | | £2 875 000 |

This net profit is a little more than double the present figure of around £1 300 000. This is due to the reduction in the rate of corporation tax from 45 per cent to $42\frac{1}{2}$ per cent in 1970.

The company's cash flow situation and the actual tax disbursements would differ substantially from the above profit and loss account because of the new tax system introduced late in 1970. Under this new tax system the company would be allowed to depreciate the new investment in plant and machinery for corporation tax purposes (if not in a development area) at an initial rate of 60 per cent for the year in which the expenditure was incurred and the balance at 25 per cent a year in subsequent years (on a declining balance basis). As the company has adequate profits from other sources to set off against the accelerated depreciation, it can be assumed that it will elect to take advantage of this for tax purposes only, while it will depreciate in the profit and loss account at the normal rate—say, a straight line 15 per cent a year. Assuming that the capital expenditure on plant and machinery is incurred in year 2, the profit and loss account over the next five years will probably appear as follows (in £ million):

| Year | 1 | 2 | 3 | 4 | 5 |
|---|---|---|---|---|---|
| Trading profits on old business | £2.1 | 2.1 | 2.1 | 2.1 | 2.1 |
| ditto on new business | — | — | 1.5 | 3.0 | 4.7 |
| Total trading profits | £2.1 | 2.1 | 3.6 | 5.1 | 6.8 |
| Less: | | | | | |
| Depreciation on old assets | 0.4 | 0.3 | 0.4 | 0.3 | 0.4 |
| Depreciation on £6m P. and M. | — | 0.9 | 0.9 | 0.9 | 0.9 |
| Depreciation on £3m bdgs. | — 0.4 | 0.1  1.3 | 0.1  1.4 | 0.1  1.3 | 0.1  1.4 |
| Gross profit | 1.7 | 0.8 | 2.2 | 3.8 | 5.4 |
| Less interest on borrowings | — | 0.2 | 0.4 | 0.4 | 0.4 |
| Profit before Corporation Tax | 1.7 | 0.6 | 1.8 | 3.4 | 5.0 |
| Less Corporation Tax | 0.7 | — | — | 1.6 | 2.4 |
| Net profit to equity | 1.0 | 0.6 | 1.8 | 1.8 | 2.6 |
| Less dividend | 1.0 | 1.0 | 1.0 | 1.0 | 1.5 |
| Retained earnings | — | (0.4) | 0.8 | 0.8 | 1.1 |

From the above proforma profit and loss account the cash accruing to the company can be built up as follows (in £ million):

| Year | 1 | 2 | 3 | 4 | 5 |
|---|---|---|---|---|---|
| Starting cash | 3.5 | — | — | — | — |
| Excess working capital | 0.5 | 1.0 | — | — | — |
| New borrowings | — | 4.3 | — | — | — |
| Depreciation | 0.4 | 1.3 | 1.4 | 1.3 | 1.4 |
| Retained profits | — | (0.4) | 0.8 | 0.8 | 1.1 |
| Total | 4.4 | 6.2 | 2.2 | 2.1 | 2.5 |

It will be seen that over the five years some £17 400 000 of cash has accumulated while the original simulation assumed that the investment would be of the order of £9 000 000. A second simulation exercise could follow, doubling in year 4 the original capital investment of £9 000 000 with the results of this further expansion appearing in year 7 or 8. However, such a rate of expansion, where each additional £9 000 000 invested gives a pre-tax predepreciation profit of £4 700 000 (50 per cent) even though this rate is reduced to something of the order of 20 per cent DCF (assuming a ten-year life of the assets and a not too rapid decline of the profitability after the peak in year 5 above is reached) would be difficult to maintain.

Such a simulation is necessary in order to convert the company's overall financial objectives into objectives which can easily be understood by line management, such as DCF return required on new investments.

*Problems of too-rapid expansion.* In profit planning there is a further complication connected with the timing and size of any new investment. A company of a certain size can only undertake new investments related to the size of the company at certain intervals of time. For example, in the case of Midland Engineering a single new investment of £17 500 000 cannot be undertaken unless it is spread over a period of five years and even then a certain profit squeeze is likely to happen between year 1 and year 2 when money is raised by borrowings and the profits from this new investment start coming in, say in year 3, as the proforma profit and loss account shows.

On the basis of the above projection, although the objectives of doubling equity profits by year 5 may have been achieved, the present dividend of 20 per cent will be uncovered in year 2 and barely covered in year 1. This is an illustration of the problems of too rapid expansion in relation to the size of the business. The alternatives are either a smaller expansion, which would not require raising loan capital, or delaying the expansion until further cash is accumulated. The objection to these alternatives is that smaller expansion might not achieve the five-year profit objective, while the delay until further cash is accumulated would increase the vulnerability of the company to a take-over bid by further increasing its holdings of idle cash.

Once this simulation exercise has been prepared it is up to the board to examine the position and weigh up the various possible alternatives and their risks before reaching a decision as to the timing and size of any expansion programme.

## 7:13 Techniques of investment appraisal

So far it has been assumed that there are always more opportunities for investment than there is money to undertake these. This should be so for any well managed company. In fact there should be a continuous flow of capital expenditure proposals originating from line management and related to the present type of business of the company as well as other proposals originating from research and development, from top management and other sources. These later proposals would possibly involve the company in new technology, new products or new geographical markets.

The purpose of investment appraisal is twofold: on the one hand to compare a number of alternative capital expenditure proposals, and on the other hand to choose a combination of these proposals to suit the profit objective of the company.

There are three recognised methods of assessing individual capital expenditure proposals:

1    Return on investments
2    Pay-back
3    Discounted cash flow (DCF)

*Return on investments.* The first method is also the simplest and the one which has traditionally been used: £10 000 is deposited with a bank or a building society and at the end of a year £600 has been credited for interest. Therefore the return is 6 per cent a year.

However, a company's investment decisions are more complex than this. Money is spent over a period of years on buildings, plant and machinery, stocks and working capital and is also recovered over these years in varying amounts by depreciation, trading profits, tax payments and receipts of government grants and in some cases subsidies, sale or liquidation of remaining assets which are not required. Also trading profits can vary from year to year. Using this method, therefore, which cannot take into account the timing of cash flows (either in or out), and must of necessity use simplifications of what is capital and what is income, is not an accurate measure of comparison between projects with different timing of the cash flows.

*Pay-back method.* In the pay-back method the cash spent in the early years and the cash received in later years are totalled. The number of years in which the total receipts equal the total payments is the pay-back period. This method does take account of the timing of the cash flows. In fact, it is specifically related to timing and may be applied to projects where there is an expenditure of cash which is followed by receipts of cash. It cannot be applied where, over a period of years, "cash in" and "cash out" alternate. It also assumes that a project with a short pay-back period is preferable to a project with a long pay-back period. This may be true in certain circumstances, such as for highly risky projects, but it does not tell us which project is more profitable.

*Discounted cash flow.* The discounted cash flow method takes cognisance of both time and profit. It is based on the premise that an investment of cash in a project is made on the expectation of receiving over a period of years enough cash not only to cover the original investment but also to yield a profit, that is, that there will be more "cash in" than "cash out." A detailed table of all the transactions involving cash or a transfer of assets from or to another use (their cash value should then be estimated) is drawn up and a net cash flow (in or out) is drawn up for the whole estimated life of the project. These cash flows are then discounted back to the starting year either at a predetermined rate of compound interest (net present value) or at the rate of interest which will equalise cash spent with cash received (internal rate of return) the formula used for discounting a sum of money $V$ at a rate of interest $r$ over $n$ years is as follows:

$$\text{Present value} = V \times (1 + r)^{-n}$$

This method takes into account the difference in time and the amount of money which this difference in time makes to a cash flow.

## 7:14 Comparison of investment appraisal methods

A simple example may illustrate the difference in the three methods. Two projects are assumed, each requiring a capital expenditure of £1000, the first (project A) with a life of four years and the second (project B) with a life of ten years. The cash outflow therefore consists in both projects of £1000 in year 0 but the cash inflows shown in a simplified manner are as follows:

| YEAR | PROJECT A | | | PROJECT B | | |
| | Depreciation | Profit | Total | Depreciation | Profit | Total |
| --- | --- | --- | --- | --- | --- | --- |
| 1 | 200 | 100 | 300 | 100 | 200 | 300 |
| 2 | 200 | 150 | 350 | 100 | 300 | 400 |
| 3 | 200 | 150 | 350 | 100 | 200 | 300 |
| 4 | 200 | 250 | 450 | 100 | 200 | 300 |
| 5 | 200 | 150 | 350 | 100 | 150 | 250 |
| 6 | | | | 100 | 100 | 200 |
| 7 | | | | 100 | 100 | 200 |
| 8 | | | | 100 | 50 | 150 |
| 9 | | | | 100 | 50 | 150 |
| 10 | | | | 100 | 50 | 150 |
| Total | 1000 | 800 | 1800 | 1000 | 1400 | 2400 |

According to the first method (return on investment) project A has a return of 16 per cent, that is £800 ÷ 5 = £160 a year, while project B has a return of 14 per cent, that is £1400 ÷ 10 = £140 a year. Therefore project A is preferable to project B.

According to the second method both projects have a pay-back period of three years and therefore on that basis the choice is indifferent.

According to the DCF method the net present value discounting at 10 per cent a year compound is as follows:

Project A: cash inflows = £1349 less cash outflow £1000 = NPV £349
Project B: cash inflows = £1596 less cash outflow £1000 = NPV £596.

Using the internal rate of return the cash inflows of project A equal £1000 at a rate of 21 per cent compound whereas those of project B equal £1000 at a rate of 25 per cent compound.

Under the more precise DCF method, which takes into account the timing of the cash flows as well as their size, project $B$ is preferable to project $A$.

Of the two projects, the second (project $B$) should therefore be selected if it is assumed either that the two projects are mutually exclusive or that the company can afford to spend only £1000 at a time. It has also been assumed that both sets of cash flow are equally certain.

When a capital expenditure proposal is put forward by management for approval by the board two opposing factors influence management's thinking:

1     The proposal must be presented in a favourable light so that it can be chosen in preference to other proposals competing for the company's limited resources

2     A proposal which is too optimistic may create unjustified expectations of performance

It is therefore desirable that all capital expenditure proposals should be assessed on similar bases: all general assumptions on the behaviour of the environment and its effects on the business should be the same for all projects.

Mathematicians distinguish between risk and uncertainty. In the case of risk the outcome is uncertain but the probabilities of any possible outcome are known. In the case of uncertainty, the probability of any particular outcome cannot be predicted. Most investment decisions are not like tossing a coin 50/50. Investment decisions are "one off" and the only certainty is that the out-turn will differ to some extent from the forecast.

*Additional advantages of DCF method.* The DCF method of investment appraisal has the added advantage that by analysing the cash flow of the proposal it is possible to test any number of possible alternative out-turns. By doing so it is possible to find which factor is of significance to the returns of the particular project. For example, it may be found that a year's delay in completing a plant and getting it into full production has a more significant effect on the profitability of a capital expenditure proposal than an increase in raw materials costs, or alternatively that a rise in labour costs is more significant than an increase in the original capital costs.

There are many computer programmes to calculate cash flows and DCF returns on which to test alternative assumptions to find out which variables are significant to the return. Ultimately management will have to take a decision based on its judgement of the uncertainty. It will have to decide for example whether the uncertainty of a year's delay in the construction and commissioning of the plant (which delay would make the proposal unattractive) is such that the project should be abandoned or not. In fact once management has been given the facts they could apply subjective probability assessments based on their knowledge of the business. The knowledge of the business would indicate which factors in the cash forecast are more uncertain than others. For example it is fairly certain that labour costs will rise over the years, that labour will be in short supply, that costs of fixed capital will also rise and that interest rates are more likely to rise than fall. What exact rates to apply to each individual factor is a matter of managerial judgement. It should be stressed, however, that such rates as are agreed should be applied uniformly to all projects so as to enable management to make a fair assessment of the relative merits of each individual project.

Ultimately the forecast cash flows of any individual project are based on forecasts of the environment and the internal company conditions. The internal situation should be under the control of management and it is their job to see that any measures necessary to adapt to changing environment are taken in time. Hence the necessity for forecasting and also for assessing all possible alternative situations which might affect the project, so as to be able to take corrective measures where necessary. For example, if completion on time is important to the profitability of a project, the management should concentrate its efforts to achieve this but should also make provisions for minimising any losses if delay does ultimately take place.

### 7:15   Planned growth by mergers or acquisition

A merger implies a voluntary amalgamation of two or more companies. An acquisition implies the purchase of one company by another. Where a company resists being acquired the term take-over is appropriate. In practice the terms of acquisition and take-over are used indiscriminately and have become interchangeable.

A merger or an acquisition may have various aims. In the context of financial planning, however, a merger or acquisition is justified only if it forms part of a programme of growth of the company. It has already been mentioned that profit should be the long term objective of a company and that under certain conditions a profit objective is difficult to achieve through the use of internal resources only (see page 194) either because the size of the next step is too large to take in one go, or because technically the change is such as to require expertise beyond that available to the management.

Earlier in this chapter the example of the Midland Engineering Company was mentioned where an investment of £17 500 000 even if spread over five years would create a profit squeeze between years 1 and 3 despite the large cash and other hidden reserves of the company. A way of overcoming this would be through an acquisition which would add immediate profits to the company. Using the example on page 197, an acquisition in year 1, for say £17 500 000, of a company making a profit of £2 000 000 before tax and depreciation would avoid the profit squeeze. The acquisition could be financed by existing cash and excess working capital £5 000 000, new long term borrowings £7 000 000, new equity £5 000 000 (1 333 333 new shares at their market value of £3.75 a share) and short term borrowings repayable over the following three years of £2 000 000. The profit and loss account would appear as follows (in £m):

| Year | 1 | 2 | 3 |
|---|---|---|---|
| Trading profit on old business | 2.1 | 2.1 | 2.1 |
| Interest on investments | 0.4 | | |
| Trading profit on acquisition | | 2.0 | 2.0 |
| Less: Depreciation on old business | 0.4 | 0.3 | 0.4 |
| Depreciation on acquisition | | 0.5 | 0.5 |
| Interest on new long term loan | | 0.7 | 0.7 |
| Interest on short term advances | | 0.2 | |
| Profit before tax | 2.1 | 2.4 | 2.5 |
| Less corporation tax | 0.9 | 1.0 | 1.0 |
| Less dividends payable | 1.0 | 1.3 | 1.3 |
| Retained earnings | 0.2 | 0.1 | 0.2 |

The cash flow of the company would appear as follows (in £m):

| | | | |
|---|---|---|---|
| Starting cash | 3.5 | 1.1 | 1.0 |
| Excess working capital | 0.5 | 1.0 | |
| Borrowing long term | 7.0 | | |
| Borrowing short term | 2.0 | | |
| New shares (1 333 333 at £3.75) | 5.0 | | |
| Retained profits | 0.2 | 0.1 | 0.2 |
| Depreciation (total) | 0.4 | 0.8 | 0.9 |
| Total cash available | 18.6 | 3.0 | 2.1 |
| Less payments: | | | |
| Purchase of new company | 17.5 | | |
| Repayment of advance | | 2.0 | |
| Cash carried forward | 1.1 | 1.0 | 2.1 |

While the above example shows that an acquisition can be an alternative method of accelerating the growth of the company beyond what would be possible from internal resources in one single step there are a number of pitfalls of which management should be aware before attempting to grow by acquisitions.

## 7:16 Problems arising from acquisitions

The word "synergy" has often been mentioned in connection with acquisitions. It implies that the company being acquired has some advantage which when added to the advantages of the purchasing company will result in a total benefit in excess of the sum total of the advantages. For example if a company owns factories with a total capacity well in excess of its market, it can buy another company in the same market, close down some of the purchased factories and increase the throughput of its own factories. Similarly if a company's own R & D effort is weak it can buy another company for the purpose of acquiring its R & D effort. However valid in theory such synergistic effects may be, in practice they present a number of problems. These are of two kinds: managerial and financial.

Basically the managerial problems revolve around the integration of a new group of people with its own way of doing things into an existing organisation and finding the right people to run the enlarged organisation. However it is with the financial problems that this chapter is concerned.

The maximum size of a company for acquisition is determined by the following criteria:

**1** Whether the acquisition is to be paid for by cash or by the issue of new shares. If the acquisition is to be paid by cash then an appraisal of both companies' cash resources is necessary so that the net cost to the purchasing company can be assessed, and the method of raising this cash can be determined.

If the acquisition is to be paid by shares, the management of the purchasing company must be satisfied that the shares of their company are not undervalued in relation to their prospects and to the shares of other companies.

**2** Whether the price to be paid for the new company is one which will help the acquiring company to achieve its profit objective. A company as a going concern represents a series of future earnings over the years and this is what the acquiring company will be paying for. The price the purchaser should be willing to pay should not exceed the minimum acceptable DCF rate of return on the expected future cash flow of the acquired company after adjusting this for the possible benefits and costs of integration within the acquiring company.

This calculation should determine the maximum price which a bidder should pay to acquire a company, with one exception: if certain assets of the company to be acquired are surplus to requirements then the realisable cash value of these assets could be added to the maximum price payable. Any price paid in excess of this maximum figure would delay instead of help to achieve the company's objective.

3 However good the estimates on the company to be acquired are, they are based on information and forecasts either supplied by the management of the company to be acquired (which may be either a willing or a reluctant seller) or obtained from outside sources. Hence such estimates are liable to a larger degree of error than estimates of the acquiring company's own business. Management will have to take a decision on the degree of confidence it has in the prepared estimates and the downward adjustment it may want to make (if any) on the maximum amount it is prepared to pay to acquire the business.

4 Finally, there may be marketing, technological or other pressing reasons why management may want to acquire that particular business and no other. The finance director may find himself under considerable pressure from other members of the management team to pay "over the odds" for the proposed acquisitions. If the company has a well defined profit growth plan which has been accepted by the board, then the finance director should point out to his colleagues the effect paying over the odds would have on the achievement of the plan.

The above points could be illustrated by assessing the maximum price a company should be prepared to pay for the Midland Engineering Company already mentioned. Let us assume that on taking the company over the purchasers would close down the existing factories, that production of centre lathes and milling machines would cease, and that radial drills and presses would be produced at their own existing plants where there is spare capacity. Assume, too, that as a result of this transfer gross margins would rise by 10 per cent and that the volume of sales of radial drills and presses would not suffer from this change of ownership.

A cash flow forecast can then be built up as follows (in £m):

| YEAR | 1 | 2 | 3 | 4 | 5 | 6 |
|---|---|---|---|---|---|---|
| Sales | 12.7 | 9.0 | 7.0 | 7.5 | 7.5 | 8.0 |
| Less cost of production | 8.1 | 5.9 | 3.5 | 3.4 | 3.4 | 3.6 |
| Gross manufacturing margin | 4.6 | 3.1 | 3.5 | 4.1 | 4.1 | 4.4 |
| Less company's existing overheads to be phased out | 2.5 | 1.5 | 0.5 | | | |
| New overheads resulting from expansion | | 0.5 | 0.7 | 1.0 | 1.0 | 1.0 |
| Cost of transfer of production | 0.5 | 0.5 | | | | |
| Net profit before tax and depreciation | 1.6 | 0.6 | 2.3 | 3.1 | 3.1 | 3.4 |
| Less estimated tax on previous year's profits | 1.0 | 0.6 | 0.2 | 0.9 | 1.3 | 1.3 |
| Plus company's surplus cash | 3.8 | | | | | |
| Sale of land and buildings | | 5.5 | | | | |
| Reduction in working capital | 0.6 | 1.0 | 0.5 | | | |
| Net cash inflow | 5.0 | 6.5 | 2.6 | 2.2 | 1.8 | 2.1 |

Let us assume that the purchasing company has an objective of a minimum return of 10 per cent a year. DCF, that it accepts the above forecast, that the years from 7 to 10 will give an annual net cash flow of £2 000 000 a year and that by the end of year 10 the residual value will be equal to the tax liability for year 10. The cash flows and their present value will then be as follows:

| YEAR | CASH FLOW | PRESENT VALUE AT 10% A YEAR |
|---|---|---|
| | £m | £m |
| 1 | 5.0 | 4.7 |
| 2 | 6.5 | 5.6 |
| 3 | 2.6 | 2.0 |
| 4 | 2.2 | 1.6 |
| 5 | 1.8 | 1.1 |
| 6 | 2.1 | 1.2 |
| 7 | 2.0 | 1.0 |
| 8 | 2.0 | 0.9 |
| 9 | 2.0 | 0.8 |
| 10 | 2.0 | 0.7 |

The present value of the total cash flow is therefore £19 600 000 and this should be the maximum price this particular purchaser should pay for the Midland Engineering Company (approximately £4 a share). If the market price of the shares is £3.87 (see page 184), the shares are fully valued in the market and it is unlikely that shareholders would be tempted to part with them at such a small premium, but if it is £2.42

(ten times earnings), shareholders could well be tempted to part with their shares at some price in excess of say £3.

## 7:17 Summary of objectives of financial planning

The purpose of financial planning is to achieve a profit objective within a specific time span by deploying the company's assets to their most profitable use. To achieve this the cash flow of the company must be forecast in detail over the next three to five years and in general outline for a longer period. The time length of this outline plan will depend upon the type of business and the liquidity or otherwise of their assets. The more difficult it is to change the use of the assets, that is, the more specific the assets are, the longer must be the time span of the outline plan.

The financial plan should determine the amount of money available from time to time for expansion, the minimum return required from any new investment, the maximum size of new investment which the company can afford at any one time, the steps it may be necessary to take to achieve a specific objective including the need for acquisitions if necessary.

The achievement of the financial plan should be closely controlled so that measures may be taken to counteract any external factors which may influence the success of the plan. Also continued monitoring is required to see that the long term cash flow objectives do not affect adversely the short term profit and loss account. It is easy to postpone the achievement of profits in order to expand the business and hopefully make profits in the future. A proper balance between the current profit and loss account and the long term expansion of the business must be kept.

# Index